THE
LAW
OF
ATTRACTION

THE
LAW
OF
ATTRACTION

||||||||||||||||||||||||||||||||||||||||||||||||||||||||||||||||||||||||||||||

THE POWER OF THOUGHT TO MANIFEST
YOUR BEST LIFE

WILLIAM WALKER ATKINSON

INTRODUCTION BY JOEL FOTINOS

REVISED AND UPDATED

ST. MARTIN'S
ESSENTIALS
NEW YORK

Published in the United States by St. Martin's Essentials,
an imprint of St. Martin's Publishing Group

INTRODUCTION Copyright © 2023 by Joel Fotinos. All rights reserved.
Printed in the United States of America. For information, address
St. Martin's Publishing Group, 120 Broadway, New York, NY 10271.

www.stmartins.com

Designed by Steven Seighman

The Library of Congress Cataloging-in-Publication Data
is available upon request.

ISBN 978-1-250-88812-9 (trade paperback)
ISBN 978-1-250-88813-6 (ebook)

Our books may be purchased in bulk for promotional, educational, or
business use. Please contact your local bookseller or the Macmillan
Corporate and Premium Sales Department at 1-800-221-7945, extension
5442, or by email at MacmillanSpecialMarkets@macmillan.com.

Originally published as *Thought Vibration or
the Law of Attraction in the Thought World* in 1906.

First St. Martin's Essentials Edition: 2023

10 9 8 7 6 5 4 3 2 1

CONTENTS

||||||||||||||||||||||||||||||||||||||||||||||||

INTRODUCTION

||||||||||||||||||||||||||||||||||||||||||||||||||

There is a good chance you have already heard of the concept "The Law of Attraction"—it's been featured in bestselling books, popular television shows, countless talks, classes, and more. That concept—that we can use our minds to help bring forth that which we want—is now very widely taught, including in the mainstream.

But have you ever wondered where we got the term "The Law of Attraction"? Or how we first came to know about it?

THE LAW OF ATTRACTION AND COMMON SENSE

Let's take a quick step back before I answer those questions. Simply put, the Law of Attraction is the idea that our thoughts create (or help to create) our reality, and that by changing our thoughts, we change our life experience. To take this one step further, there are two main levels of concept.

First is the common-sense level—if you think positive thoughts and adopt a positive outlook it makes sense that you will have a more positive life experience. And the reverse is also true—if you habitually think negative thoughts and adopt a negative outlook, you'll probably have a more negative life experience.

In other words, what we choose to focus on becomes an indicator of the experience we have.

For instance, two similar people who have similar events happen to them can have very different *experiences* of that event based on their outlook (as well as other factors, of course). As a very broad, general example, let's say these two people were both let go from their jobs. The negative-thinking person can see this as confirmation that life never works out for them, or that their boss was toxic and had it in for them, or that they were never appreciated, or even turn to fear of how they are going to pay rent, etc. Those may all be true. The positive-thinking person can see this as a sign of a new beginning, they should do something different with their life, a signal to pursue a different path, or perhaps even a valuable learning lesson in improving their work performance in future jobs. Those may also all be true.

If both of those can be true, it would follow that our positivity or negativity can be a major factor in what we attract to us.

Popular psychology will tell us that the way we experience our life is often largely determined by *how we frame the experiences* we have in life. Neither the optimist nor pessimist is wrong, it's just a different way of viewing what happens to us. And common sense would also suggest—at least to me—that the more we see what happens to us in a positive way, as much as possible at least, that we'll probably open ourselves up to more positive experiences along the way. When we are open and positive, we tend to see more possibilities, and have more inclination to pursue those possibilities. Of course, reframing our thoughts and experiences can be more difficult than we realize, but the effort is usually worth it.

THE NEW THOUGHT PHILOSOPHY

The second level of this thinking has a more deeply spiritual and philosophical basis. Around the end of the nineteenth and early twentieth centuries, a philosophy known as New Thought began to gain popularity. New Thought grew out of the Transcendentalist movement, as well as a few other schools of thought, and became known under a number of names, such as "Mental Science." Early teachers began to create organizations and churches that espoused this philosophy, including Charles and Myrtle Fillmore (the Unity movement) and Ernest Holmes (the Institute of Religious Science, which has gone through several name changes, most recently as Centers for Spiritual Living). There were New Thought seminaries, publishers, magazines, and correspondence courses. The movement was heavily influenced by women and by the social issues of the time, including abolition and child labor.

New Thought teaches a number of tenets, one of which is the idea of what Ernest Holmes called The One Mind, or Atkinson in this book calls The Absolute. This is the idea that there are not two powers in the Universe—God and Satan, good and evil, heaven and hell—but rather there is one creative power that has created all life. The ideas of duality are our own invention and states of mind that we experience here on earth. This power—be it called God, Life, Spirit, the Universe, Power, etc.—has created all life, including the life of you and of me.

New Thought teaches that when one realizes they are created in the image of this Power, they then can realize they are one with the Power that created them (made in Its image). And then they can realize that the creative process of this Power is available to them through the use of their thoughts. Most New Thought teachers will teach (in their own language) that "thoughts are things," that thoughts have creative power. New Thought endeavors to teach people how to use their mind creatively to improve their life experience. This can mean to experience more love, peace, joy, etc., or to experience greater abundance of finances, ideas, creativity, etc. Because we are made from Spirit, we are "divine heirs" of the infinite power and abundance of Spirit.

(Since this is just an introduction to The Law of Attraction and not a book about the history and ideas of New Thought, I've given you only a very quick overview and generalization of this New Thought concept—just a taste—though the philosophy has much more to offer. To learn more about the philosophy itself, you can read classic New Thought books such as *The Science of Mind* by Ernest Holmes, *The Edinburgh Lectures* by Thomas Troward, or *The Game of Life and How to Play It* by Florence Scovel Shinn, to name just a few.)

"THE LAW OF ATTRACTION" EMERGES

It was in these early teachings that the phrase "the law of attraction" was first used, at least in printed materials. Early

New Thought teachers Prentice Mulford and Ralph Waldo Trine both use the phrase "the law of attraction" in their writings. Many other early teachers wrote about it without calling it "the law of attraction" specifically. So this concept was in the zeitgeist of the time.

In 1906, Atkinson published a book titled, *Thought Vibration or the Law of Attraction in the Thought World*. As far as I can tell, William Walker Atkinson was the first teacher/author to use the term "the Law of Attraction" in a book title and as the basic concept for an entire book. That is the book you are now holding, though with the simplified title *The Law of Attraction*. Many others after Atkinson went on to use the phrase and concept of the Law of Attraction, and the concept gained considerable attention in the early 2000s, a century after Atkinson's book, with authors such as Rhonda Byrne (*The Secret*) and Wayne Dyer (*You See It When You Believe It*).

KEYS CONCEPTS IN THIS BOOK

You'll see as you read the book that there are several themes that Atkinson stresses. Here are just a few:

- *Magnetizing yourself*—learning the process to move to the vibration where you are attracting what you want
- *The Absolute*—Atkinson often uses this phrase to refer to the Higher Power, God, the Universe, the Creator, the One Mind, or whatever else you might call it
- *Will and Will Power*—will is what you want, and will power is consistently taking actions toward what you want, even when it's difficult to do so

- *Strong Desire*—Atkinson is clear that you must intensely love the thing you want in order to become an attractor of that thing (whether it is a quality, like peace or love, or an experience, like a new job or relationship, or a thing, like a home or car)
- *Conscious and subconscious mind*—Atkinson uses these terms similarly to the way we think of them today—the conscious mind is the mind we think with, and the subconscious mind is the place where our memories and preferences and experiences are all stored, and it is creative
- *Auto-suggestion*—using specific thoughts deliberately to plant those seeds into our creative subconscious mind, to help become magnetized and thus reach our goal
- *Singular focus on the goal*—Atkinson tells us it is more effective to put our energy toward one main goal, rather than to dissipate our energy toward several goals

A BIT ABOUT THE BOOK

Let me mention a few thoughts about this book. First, I truly wish I had been Atkinson's editor for *The Law of Attraction*. The self-help movement that we are familiar with in our present time wasn't the same as it was when Atkinson wrote this book. Today most self-help books have some similar structures— each chapter is a main idea that builds on the previous one, and chapters might have exercises or practices, often at the end of the chapter. Some are even workbooks, where there is space to write in answers to questions the author poses. On the other hand, I've read many early self-help books from the late 1800s and early 1900s, and they tend to not be as structured. That isn't to say this book doesn't have a structure—it does—it's just not as linear as most books today, and it can be a bit stream of consciousness at times. If I had been his editor, I would have streamlined the book, added some chapters with practical suggestions and more stories from the author's life (and those of his students), and have the author add practical suggestions in each chapter.

But the book is a product of its time. Atkinson's voice in the book is of a straight-talking mentor—not as a guru, as he is quick to point out. He wants to tell it like it is, at least from his point of view. Although that means it doesn't quite follow the same structure of today's self-help books, it also has a certain charm that comes from the time period it's written in. It's a bit more formal than today's self-help books tend to be, and also bolder in its announcements and ideas. Perhaps today's writers see more nuances in both their ideas and audiences than writers in the past, I'm not sure.

Atkinson also repeats a number of his ideas over and over. Again, a modern editor would have helped streamline this. On the other hand, I find the repetition can be helpful to make sure the ideas he repeats sink in. Sometimes—at least for me, and I'm assuming I'm not alone—I need an idea to be repeated so that I can not only grasp its meaning, but also its importance.

You'll notice that we are referring to this book as revised for the twenty-first century. What this means is that I went through the text and made changes that will help modern readers. Those changes are mainly in the areas of capitalization, outdated terms, and adding a few explanatory words/phrases here and there. None of the revisions changed any meaning the author intended, and none of the changes were substantive. This was merely to do some "nips and tucks" here and there, so that the text's ideas weren't obscured for the reader because of outdated wordage or grammar. But it's important to point out that you are reading Atkinson's book—his full book—with just a few adjustments for the modern reader.

WHO WAS WILLIAM WALKER ATKINSON?

Note: I've written about Atkinson before, most recently in the introduction to a collection of Atkinson books called *The Secrets of Mind Power*. The section below is adapted from that introduction.

William Walker Atkinson might be the most famous and influential inspirational writer you have never heard of. I say that because Atkinson at one time was extremely popular, but somehow while his ideas have continued to flourish, his name has been largely forgotten. With one exception (which I'll mention later), his books are difficult to find, relegated to print-on-demand status. It is my hope that this volume will bring some of Atkinson's most potent and timeless ideas to many new readers. He deserves a wide readership. Atkinson was a lawyer, author, publisher, editor, and speaker. Born in Baltimore in 1862, Atkinson married Margaret Foster Black, had two children, became a lawyer, and moved to Chicago. That last sentence sums up years of his life in just a few words, but there is much about Atkinson that we do not know. What we do know, mostly through his articles and writings, is that at one point his life took a difficult turn. He suffered a physical and emotion breakdown, as well as financial ruin. It was then that he found books on mental healing. Chicago at that time was a hot spot for the fast-growing New Thought philosophy, the philosophy based on transcendentalism as well as mesmerism and mental science. He studied with two of New Thought's most formidable and influential leaders, Helen Wilmans and Emma Curtis Hopkins. His mind, body, and finances were all healed using the ideas from New Thought. He began writing articles about his experiences and about the metaphysical ideas that he now embraced. And shortly after that, he began writing books. He also began working with several New Thought magazines, including *New Thought* magazine, *Advanced Thought*, and eventually *Nautilus* magazine, which was founded and headed by early New Thought publisher Elizabeth Towne.

Eventually he began to publish books through his own publishing companies, the Yogi Publication Society and Advance Thought Publishing Company. Here's where his story gets interesting, at least to me. Atkinson was incredibly prolific, and he wrote many books about his main interests, which included mental science, New Thought, psychic studies, numerology, the occult, natural health and wellness, and also Eastern philosophy, especially Hinduism, which he had become interested in. During his lifetime, he wrote well over a hundred books, which is a remarkable achievement.

However, instead of just publishing them all under his own name, he evidently created a series of pseudonyms, each with a different emphasis. For example, the books under his own name dealt with mental sciences, the occult, divination, and spiritual success. His books with Eastern and Hindu influences were written under the name Swami Ramacharaka. He also published under the names Swami Bhakta Vishita and Swami Panchadasi, and these were largely about clairvoyance, psychic thought, and life after death. Under his pseudonym Theron Q. Dumont, he focused on mental power, self-improvement, self-confidence, memory, and concentration. The health and wellness titles were published under the name of Theodore Sheldon, and the esoteric studies, such as Rosicrucianism, were published with the name Magus Incognito. There were other pseudonyms as well.

Notice that I said he evidently published books with pseudonyms. He never revealed one way or another if he authored those, and in fact even created elaborate stories of who some of these "authors" were. However, there doesn't seem to be evidence of these "other" authors actually existing. Not to mention, those books all had the same "feel" as the books published under his own name. It is now widely accepted that he was the author of the books under these pseudonyms. His most famous pseudonym was "the Three Initiates," who authored a book that claimed to be of authentic Hermetic wisdom, called *The Kybalion*. This book ended up being his bestseller, the book that he is best known for today, though most readers of the book don't know that the name of the author is actually William Walker Atkinson. There is some question as to the authorship, whether he wrote the book by himself, or with others, or even at all, but careful study of *The Kybalion* reveals that there is a vast probability that Atkinson was the sole author of the book. (*The Kybalion* is available as a part of the Essential Wisdom

Library series from St. Martin's Essentials, with a foreword by me as well).

While his pseudonyms are fascinating, the books he wrote under his own name are equally fascinating. Many of his other ideas are now commonplace as well, and some are still ahead of their time. This book showcases a man with a brilliant mind and charismatic personality. Although the language is of the times when he wrote them, his ideas are timely and practical and valuable. You can tell as you read this book that he truly wants to help the reader improve their life. He writes in a motivational, personal style, totally graspable and applicable for the modern reader.

Yes, some of the stories or examples are dated, but the ideas behind those examples transcend the time he wrote them. After all, Atkinson would be the first to tell us that he didn't invent these ideas, he only wrote about them in a way that made them understandable. His confidence in and love of the ideas in his books burst forth form every paragraph. Reading his book is more than instructional, it is joyful. In Atkinson's later years, he become involved in the International New Thought Alliance, and in fact was their president at one point. He ran his publishing businesses, remained an active lawyer, popular speaker, and influential New Thought teacher. He died in 1932, just shy of his seventieth birthday. His publishing company continued to publish his books for decades, but otherwise he left behind no organization or "center" that taught his principles and ideas.

Perhaps that is why his name isn't well known in this time. His books didn't have an author or organization to keep them fresh in the minds of readers. However, as you read any of his books, you'll begin to see his ideas, from these books written more than a century ago, in today's current bestsellers. Whenever I notice it, I pause and smile, knowing that Atkinson's influence is still being felt today.

IT'S YOUR TURN

It's your turn to discover Atkinson and his book *The Law of Attraction*. You have somehow attracted the book to you, so my guess is that there is something in this book that will be impactful for you. Read through it, try to grasp the idea of what he is saying, and then work to apply those ideas to your own life.

We are all ultimately the author of our own experience, and I hope that this author, William Walker Atkinson, inspires you to write a glorious future, one where you attract great experiences and success.

—Joel Fotinos

PREFACE

||||||||||||||||||||||||||||||||||||||||||||||||

n December 1901, William Walker Atkinson, in assuming
the editorship of the popular magazine *New Thought*, intro-
duced himself to the readers of that periodical in a memo-
rable article. That article contained a clear, ringing, forceful
statement of his individual creed, that which nothing can af-
ford a deeper insight into the character and inner self of the
man whose name appears as author of this book. It is the crys-
tallized expression of the world-principles, the truths, which
his writings seek to illuminate, and in my opinion should be
read by every student of his works, as the key to the philosophy he teaches.

For this reason there has been attached to this, his latest
book, under the title "My Working Creed," the most vital of
the fundamental beliefs enunciated by Mr. Atkinson in that
famous introductory statement of 1901. None can read the
recurring, ringing "I BELIEVE" of this author, without feeling an answering thrill of exaltation and power. To those who

read this book I would say, imbue yourself thoroughly with the broad and beautiful spirit of those few preliminary paragraphs that you may pass on understandingly to the perusal of the teachings which follow.

Those who have an opportunity to refer to the article, which was included in "New Thought Annual for 1902" (published by The New Thought Publishing Co.), from which this Creed is taken, should do so. It tells of the work, the material success, followed by over-strain, physical and mental breakdown and financial disaster, which marked the earlier years of William Walker Atkinson. It shows how he came to know what he now holds to be the Truth, and how, in his own life, he has demonstrated its value. For from mental and physical wreck and financial ruin, he wrought through its principles, perfect health, mental vigor, and material prosperity.

Mr. Atkinson, during the many years of his connection with the magazine, *New Thought*, built for himself an enduring place in the hearts of its readers. For four years his literary work was confined to its pages (including in addition, three books for its publishers), and article after article of wonderful strength and vital force flowed from his pen. During this time several series of "lessons" appeared, under varying titles, in regard to the application of the Law of Attraction in the Thought World, lessons which created a sensation and exerted a wonderful influence upon the lives of those who applied their principles. They were written in Mr. Atkinson's own sparkling, intimate style, teeming with thought, force, energy, fire, but shorn of all atmosphere of the study, all attempt at "fine writing," polished periods or dignified metaphor, and all affectation or assumption of superior learning. One of Mr. Atkinson's cardinal principles is "Stand on your own feet," and he denounces any attempt to read infallibility into his writings. For this reason we have again prefaced the present work with a "Foreword" in which he seeks to instill into all students of New Thought, whether as expressed in his writings or in those of others, the quality of self-dependence. A reading of this Foreword will give the student a clear idea of the attitude of mind in which Mr. Atkinson thinks this and all other individual interpretations of life should be approached.

With "My Working Creed" and the "Foreword" as guides, the present reader should enter upon *The Law of Attraction*, the book proper, in a spirit calculated to extract the greatest possible value.

The Law of Attraction embraces two series of the vital lessons mentioned above, with some additional articles by Mr. Atkinson following out the same line of teaching. The order of the lessons has been somewhat changed in the combination; and for further continuity and clearness, new lesson titles in the form of chapter headings have been selected. The publishers have preferred to retain the familiar unstudied style of the lessons, as originally written, rather than to subject the articles to the literary revision by the author, which usually precedes publication in book form. They contend that Mr. Atkinson's mightiest influence, his greatest strength and power, lies in his simple, straightforward, and at times even colloquial language—the kind which "even my little son can understand," as wrote in gratitude one earnest student. It is such writing that the world needs, writing which can be read and understood by the people around the world, whether they are children or as adults. There is a great deal of so-called "fine writing" on New Thought subjects, beautiful sentences full of high, though sometimes misty thought; but this world needs common, practical, everyday application of this thought. Where there is one reader for the literary masterpiece, there are a hundred readers (plus even that other one), for the book written as a keen, live, human talks and writes about the difficulties, the problems, the possibilities of the average citizen of the world.

This is a truth Mr. Atkinson has mastered, and it is with intention he casts from him the restrictions of an academic style. He speaks, always, not in dignified tones to "the public," but in the language of a friend to YOU. It can be said of him in praise, as of another before him: *"The common people heard him gladly!"* (Mark 12:37)—the highest, most enduring tribute that can be paid to a leader.

Recognition is due to Louise Radford Wells for the revision of the proofs of this book, the selection of its title and chapter headings, and the ordered arrangement of the lessons.

—Franklin L. Berry

Editor of *New Thought* Magazine
June 15, 1906
Chicago, Illinois

FOREWORD

||||||||||||||||||||||||||||||||||||||||||||||||||||||

I am in receipt of a letter from an earnest student of New Thought, who writes me that he is endeavoring to put into practice the teachings for which I stand. That is all right—I think he will get some good out of the practice (I know that *I* do). But here is where the trouble comes in—he goes on to say that he is "a faithful disciple" of mine, and is content to "sit at the feet of the Teacher." Now, if you will pardon the slang, I must say that such talk "makes me tired." I wish no "disciples"—disciples are mere parrots repeating what one says—mere human sheep trotting along after some conceited old bellwether. I do not wish to pose as a bellwether, nor do I wish a flock of human sheep trotting after me. I want every one of my fellow students of Mental Science to be their own bellwether. I like comradeship and mutual help—the help of interdependence. But I don't like this talk of master and disciple—of leader and follower—this talk and idea of dependence.

As for sitting at any one's feet, the idea arouses all the spirit of independence within me. I don't want to sit at anyone's feet—and I don't want anyone to sit at mine. I am willing, and often glad, to listen to some teacher and to pick from their teachings such bits of truth as my mind is ready to receive. I am willing to say "I don't know," and to accept from others that which appeals to me as truth; not because the other says that it is truth, but because my mind recognizes it as such. I take my own wherever I find it, because I recognize it as mine. I know that all students and teachers get their knowledge from the only source of supply—they can't get it from anywhere else. And if some other person happens to see a particular bit of truth before I do, I gladly accept a portion of it from their hands, be they royalty or beggar; while if I happen to see the thing first, I will gladly share it with all who are ready for it, and who may want it, without feeling that I am a "leader," or "teacher," or that they are "followers" or "disciples." We are all fellow students—that's all. I recognize no one as my master—and I spurn the person who would call me "Master," if there be any so foolish. This feet-sitting talk makes me very, very weary.

I am fully aware that certain teachers convey the idea that they are chosen mouthpieces of the Infinite, and that all true teachings must bear their trademark. And I also know the fanatical devotion and bigotry that many of the followers of such teachers manifest. But this is all child's play. Those teachers sooner or later will be brought up against good hard stone walls, and their egos will be bruised until they realize "just where they are at." And the "disciples" will have some individuality knocked into them later on, and will be made to stand upon their own feet, by reason of the props being knocked from under them. The New Thought aims at making *individuals*, not at converting people into droves of sheep, following the tinkle of the bell of some conceited bellwether, who imagines that they are the Whole Thing.

> *The growing soul must realize that it has within itself all that it requires.*

The growing soul must realize that it has within itself all that it requires. It may gladly accept from other's suggestions, advice, bits of knowledge, and the like, as it goes along—the soul itself being the only judge of what it requires at each particular stage. But, in the end, it must do its own work, and must stand on its own feet. All the teachings in the world will not help you, unless you take hold of the matter yourself and work out your own salvation. You cannot get true mental or spiritual teaching by simply paying so much for a course of lessons, and doing nothing yourself. You must bring something to the teacher before you can take anything away. You must work up to an understanding before the teachings of another will do you any good.

> *The teacher may make a suggestion that will open up a line of thought for you, or they may point out a way that has proved of value to them; and thus save you much time and trouble. But you must do the real work yourself.*

The teacher may make a suggestion that will open up a line of thought for you, or they may point out a way that has proved of value to them; and thus save you much time and trouble. But you must do the real work yourself.

A teacher may be so filled with the truth that they will

overflow, and you will get some of the overflow. I believe that truth is "catching." But even so, unless you make that truth your own by living it out, and applying it to your needs, it will do you no good. And so long as you are content to "sit at their feet," and do the "disciple" act, you will not grow one inch. You will be merely a reflection of the teacher, instead of being an individual.

We need a jogging up on this point every once in a while, "lest we forget." It is so easy to have your thoughts predigested for you by some teacher or writer—so easy to receive your teaching in capsules. It is so nice to be able to sit down and swallow the summation that the teacher or writer kindly has prepared for you, and imagine that you are getting the real thing. But I tell you, friends—*it won't do the work*. Imbibe all the teachings you please, but you have got to get down to business yourself. You can't give someone else a power of attorney to do the work in your place. Life accepts no substitutes—you must step out yourself. It is mighty easy—this idea of paying so much, in time or money, to some teacher or writer, and then sneaking into the Kingdom of Heaven holding on to their skirts—but it won't work. You've got to do some hustling on your own account, and don't you make any mistake about this fact.

> *Don't suppose that you must be able to solve all the Riddles of the Universe before you can do anything.*

Many of you are running around after teachers, preachers, prophets, seers, "illuminated souls," and what not, expecting that your little fee for courses of lessons, private teachings, and all the rest, is going to land you right up in the front rank.

Don't you believe a word of it. You've got to go through the motions yourself, before you will attain anything. You can't sneak in that way—it won't work. I look around me and see many of these poor creatures "sitting at the feet" of someone or other, sinking their individuality in that of the teacher, and not daring to think an original thought—lest it conflict with some notion of their "Master." These good souls are so full of the teaching they are imbibing, they will repeat it by the yard, phrase after phrase, like a well-trained parrot. But they don't understand a bit of it. They are like the moon, which shines by reason of the reflection of the sun's rays, and has no light or heat of its own. The talk of these "disciples" and "sitters-at-the-feet" is nothing but moonshine—mere reflected light. Moons are dead, cold things—no light—no heat—no fire—no energy. Dead, dead, dead—cold, barren and "played-out." Stop this moon business and build yourself up into a Sun. You have it in you—manifest it. Start yourself in motion, and manifest Life. Don't suppose that you must be able to solve all the Riddles of the Universe before you can do anything. Never mind about those riddles, just you get down to the task that lies ahead of you, and throw into it some of that Great Life Principle that is within you waiting for a chance to manifest itself. Don't make the mistake of supposing that this or that teacher has solved the Great Riddle. If anyone says they have, they are only bluffing and whistling to keep up courage. They may have found a good-sized chunk of the truth, and if they are willing to pass you a bit of it, all right, but they don't have the Whole Thing, by a mighty sight. The Whole Thing isn't placing itself in the exclusive control of any little bit of itself. No one has a monopoly of knowing—a corner on the Truth. It is yours as much as anybody's—but you must dig for it.

Don't bother about the theories, or the unsolvable riddles—just get down to business and begin to Live. Sometimes I amuse myself by reading some of the theories and "explanations" of those who think that they have hold of the Whole Thing. After I get through with the theories of one "dead-sure" person, I take up the directly opposite theories of another person who considers themselves to be the special mouthpiece of the Absolute. Whew! It's a great brain-shaker. If you're not careful you will find yourself being served a nice dish of scrambled brains. When I get sort of "stewed-up" over such things I go out into the sun and fall back on the "Laughing Philosophy," which soon brings me around all right. Nothing will puncture these bubbles so quickly as a good dose of Laughter. Laughter is the only thing that keeps humanity from madness. The sense of humor is God's best gift to humankind. Try it the next time you get "wound up" with "high statements," "basic truths," "self-evident principles." Beware of any teachings that will not stand the test of the sunny out-of-doors, and the application of the Laughing Philosophy. Shun the teachings that require a pursed-up mouth, and a strained, preternaturally sober face. Have nothing to do with teachings that require a dim, dark, sunless room to be absorbed in—beware of teachings and doctrines that bear the musty smell of the cell upon them. Carry out into the sun the teachings that are offered you, and see whether or not they fade—apply some laughter to it, and see whether the teachings survive. Remember this test when you are perplexed or worried over some strange theory or doctrine—no matter from whence it comes. If anyone tells you that which will not bear the test—discard the teaching, for it is false in that event. Try this on my writings as well, along with the others.

Stop being a moon. Stop living by the reflected light of others. Get into action and convert yourself into a living sun. You can do it. It is within your power. Every human soul contains within it the elements of the Sun—get to work and express yourself. Stiffen up your backbone and hold your head high. Don't be afraid to say "I am IT."

This is a straight-from-the-shoulder talk. Don't tell me that you are "disciples" of mine; I refuse to have disciples. Don't try to "sit at my feet"—if you do, I will use my feet to push you off the platform. I need room to swing my feet about and don't want people sitting there. But if you wish to call me "Brother," or "Fellow Student," or "Schoolmate in the Kindergarten of God," I will be glad to have you do so. That's all we are, after all—little babes tugging away at the breast of the Absolute.

—William Walker Atkinson

MY WORKING CREED

||||||||||||||||||||||||||||||||||||||||||||||||||

I believe that each of our minds contains the greatest of all forces—that Thought is one of the greatest manifestations of energy.

I believe that the person who understands the use of Thought-force can make of themself practically what they will.

I believe that not only is one's body subject to the control of the mind, but that, also, one may change their environment, their "luck," or their circumstances, by positive thought taking the place of negative. I know that the "I Can and I Will" attitude will carry one forward to the Success level, that will seem miraculous to those on the "I Can't" level.

I believe that "thoughts are things," and that the Law of Attraction in the thought world will draw to one just what they desire or fear.

I believe in the gospel of work—in "hustling."

I believe in the I DO, as well as the I AM. I know that the one who will take advantage of the Power of the Mind, and who will manifest that power in action, will go forward to Success as surely and as steadily as the arrow from the bow of the skilled archer.

I believe in the Unity of Humankind.

I believe in being Kind.

I believe in everyone minding their own business—and allowing everyone else the same privilege. I believe that we have no right to condemn—"let the one who is without sin cast the first stone."

I believe that the one who hates is like an assassin; that the one who covets is like a thief; that the one who lusts is like an adulterer; that the gist of a crime is in its desire. Seeing this—looking into our own hearts—how can we condemn?

I believe that evil is but ignorance.

I believe that "to know all is to forgive all."

I believe that there is good in everyone; let us help each other to manifest it.

I believe in the absolute equality of all humans.

I believe in the sacredness of sex—but I also believe that sex manifests on the Spiritual and Mental planes as well as on the Physical. And I believe that all things are pure to those who are pure.

I believe that we are immortal—that the Real Self is Spirit, which uses mind and body as its tools, and manifests itself according to the fitness of the tools.

I believe that humanity is rapidly growing into a new plane of consciousness, in which we will know ourself as we are—and will recognize the I AM—the Something Within.

I believe that there is an Infinite Power in, and of, all things.

I believe that, although today we have but the faintest idea of that Power, still we will steadily grow to comprehend it more *fully—will get in closer touch with it. Even now we have momentary glimpses of its existence—a momentary consciousness of Oneness with the Absolute.*

I believe that the greatest happiness consists in maintaining toward the Absolute the attitude of the trusting child, who, feeling no doubt of the parent's love—no doubt of his wisdom— places their little hand in that of the parent, and says "Lead Thou me on."

I believe that those who feel towards the Absolute, the trustfulness of the babe which places its little tired head close to the breast of the mother, will also be conscious of the tender answering pressure, as the babe is drawn just a little closer to the mother-heart.

—William Walker Atkinson

1

THE LAW OF ATTRACTION
IN THE THOUGHT WORLD

||||||||||||||||||||||||||||||||||||||||||||||||

The Universe is governed by Law—one great Law. Its manifestations are multiform, but viewed from the Ultimate there is but *one* Law. We are familiar with some of its manifestations, but are almost totally ignorant of certain others. Still we are learning a little more every day—the veil is being gradually lifted.

We speak knowledgeably of the Law of Gravitation, but then ignore that equally wonderful manifestation, The Law of Attraction in the Thought World. We are familiar with that wonderful manifestation of Law which draws and holds together the atoms of which matter is composed—we recognize the power of the law that attracts bodies to the earth, that holds the circling worlds in their places, but we close our eyes to *the mighty Law of Attraction that draws to us the things we desire or fear, that makes or limits our lives.*

When we come to see that Thought is a force—a manifestation of energy—having a magnet-like power of attraction, we will begin to understand the why and wherefore of many things that have heretofore seemed dark to us. There is no study that will so well repay the student for their time and trouble as the study of the workings of this mighty law of the world of Thought—the Law of Attraction.

Whenever we think a thought, we are sending out vibrations which are as real as the vibrations manifesting light, heat, electricity, magnetism. That these vibrations are not evident to our five senses is no proof that they do not exist. A powerful magnet will send out vibrations and exert a force sufficient to attract to itself a piece of steel weighing a hundred pounds, but we can neither see, taste, smell, hear nor feel the mighty force. These thought vibrations, likewise, cannot be seen, tasted, smelled, heard, nor felt in the ordinary way; although it is true there are on record case studies of persons peculiarly sensitive to psychic impressions who have perceived powerful thought-waves. Also, many of us can testify that we have distinctly *felt* the thought vibrations of others, both while in the presence of the sender and also at a distance. Telepathy and its kindred phenomena are not idle dreams.

Light and heat are manifested by vibrations of a far lower intensity than those of Thought, but the difference is solely in the rate of vibration. The records of science throw an interesting light upon this question. Prof. Elisha Gray, an eminent scientist, says in his little book, "The Miracles of Nature" (or "Nature's Miracles"):

"There is much food for speculation in the thought that there exist sound-waves that no human ear can hear, and color-waves of light that no eye can see. The long, dark, soundless space between 40,000 and 400,000,000,000,000 vibrations per second, and the infinity of range beyond 700,000,000,000,000 vibrations per second, where light ceases, in the universe of motion, makes it possible to indulge in speculation."

M. M. Williams, in his work entitled "Short Chapters in Science," says:

"There is no gradation between the most rapid undulations or tremblings that produce our sensation of sound, and the slowest of those which give rise to our sensations of gentlest warmth. There is a huge gap between them, wide enough to include another world of motion, all lying between our world of sound and our world of heat and light; and there is no good reason whatever for supposing that matter is incapable of such intermediate activity, or that such activity may not give rise to intermediate sensations, provided there are organs for taking up and sensifying their movements."

I cite the above authorities merely to give you food for thought, not to attempt to demonstrate to you the fact that thought vibrations exist. The last-named fact has been fully established to the satisfaction of numerous investigators of the subject, and a little reflection will show you that it coincides with your own experiences.

We often hear repeated the well-known Mental Science statement, "Thoughts are Things," and we say these words over without consciously realizing just what is the meaning of the statement. If we fully comprehended the truth of the statement and the natural consequences of the truth back of it, we should understand many things which have appeared unclear to us, and would be able to use the wonderful power, Thought Force, just as we use any other manifestation of Energy.

As I have said, when we think we then set thought vibrations into motion at a very high degree, *"just as real as the vibrations of light, heat, sound, electricity."* And when we understand the laws governing the production and transmission of these vibrations we will be able to use them in our daily life, just as we do the better known forms of energy. Even though we cannot see, hear, weigh, or measure these vibrations is not proof that they do not exist. There exist waves of sound which no human ear can hear, although some of these are undoubtedly registered by the ear of some of the insects, and others are caught by delicate scientific instruments invented by humans; yet there is a great gap between the sounds registered by the most delicate instrument and the limit which our mind, reasoning by analogy, knows to be the boundary line between sound-waves and some other forms of vibration. And there are light waves which human eyes do not register, some of which may be detected by more delicate instruments, and many more so fine that the instrument has not yet been invented which will detect them, although improvements are being made every year and the unexplored field gradually lessened.

As new instruments are invented, new vibrations are registered by them—*and yet the vibrations were just as real before the invention of the instrument as afterward.* Supposing that we had no instruments to register *magnetism*—one might be justified in denying the existence of that particular mighty force, because it could not be tasted, felt, smelt, heard, seen, weighed, or measured. And yet the mighty magnet would still send out waves of force sufficient to draw to it pieces of steel weighing hundreds of pounds.

Each form of vibration requires its own form of instrument for action. At present the human brain seems to be the only instrument capable of registering thought-waves, although metaphysicians say that in this century scientists will invent ways to catch and register such impressions. To those who have experimented along the lines of practical telepathy, no further proof is required than the results of their own experiments.

> *Not only do our thought-waves influence ourselves and others, but they have a drawing power—they attract to us the thoughts of others, things, circumstances, people, "luck," in accord with the character of the thought uppermost in our minds.*

We are sending out thoughts of greater or lesser intensity all the time, and we are reaping the results of such thoughts. Not only do our thought-waves influence ourselves and others, but they have a drawing power—they attract to us the thoughts of others, things, circumstances, people, "luck," in accord with the character of the thought uppermost in our minds. Thoughts of Love will attract to us the Love of others; circumstances and surroundings in accord with the thought; people who are of like thought. Thoughts of Anger, Hate, Envy, Malice, and Jealousy will draw to us the foul results of kindred thoughts emanating from the minds of others. Those who think vile thoughts of others will receive them in turn from others. A strong thought, or a thought long continued, will make us the center of attraction for the corresponding thought-waves of others. Like attracts like in the Thought World—as ye sow so shall ye reap. Birds of a feather flock together in the Thought World—curses, like chickens, come home to roost, and they bring their friends with them.

> ### *Like attracts like in the Thought World—as ye sow so shall ye reap.*

The person who is filled with Love will then see Love everywhere, and will attract the Love of others. The person with Hate in their heart will then get all the Hate they can stand. One who thinks Fight generally runs up against all the Fight they want before they get through. And so it goes, each gets what they call for over the wireless telegraphy of the Mind. The one who rises in the morning feeling "grumpy" usually manages to have the whole family in the same mood before the breakfast is over. The "nagging" person generally finds enough to further gratify their "nagging" propensity during the day.

This matter of Thought Attraction is a serious one. When you stop to think about it, you will see that we really make our own surroundings, although we sometimes blame others for it. I have known people who understood this law to hold a positive, calm thought and be absolutely unaffected by the negativity surrounding them. They were like the vessel from which the oil had been poured on the troubled waters—they rested safely and calmly whilst the tempest raged around them. One is not at the mercy of the fitful storms of Thought after they have learned the workings of the Law.

We have passed through the age of physical force on to the age of intellectual supremacy, and we are now entering a new and almost unknown field, that of psychic power. This field of energy has its established laws, as well, just as the other fields have, and we should acquaint ourselves with these laws or we will be lost in the crowded area with those who don't understand how the law works. I will try to make these great underlying principles of this new field of energy, which are opening up before us, plain to you This way, you may be able to make use of this great power, and then apply it for legitimate and worthy purposes.

2

THOUGHT-WAVES AND THEIR PROCESS OF REPRODUCTION

||||||||||||||||||||||||||||||||||||||||||||||||||||

L ike a stone thrown into the water, thought produces ripples and waves which spread out over the great ocean of thought. There is this difference, however: the waves on the water move only on a level plane in all directions, whereas thought-waves move in all directions from a common center, just as do the rays from the sun.

Just as on earth we are surrounded by a great sea of air, so are we surrounded by a great sea of Mind. Our thought-waves move through this vast mental ether, extending in all directions, becoming somewhat lessened in intensity according to the distance traversed, because of the friction occasioned by the waves coming in contact with the great body of Mind surrounding us on all sides.

These thought-waves have other qualities differing from the waves on the water. *They have the property of reproducing them-*

selves. In this respect they resemble sound-waves rather than waves upon the water. Just as a note of the violin will cause the thin glass to vibrate and "sing," so will a strong thought tend to awaken similar vibrations in minds attuned to receive it. Many of the "stray thoughts" which come to us are but reflections or answering vibrations to some strong thought sent out by others. But unless our minds are attuned to receive it, the thought will not likely affect us. If we are thinking high and great thoughts, our minds acquire a certain level that corresponds to the character of the thoughts we have been thinking. And, this level once established, we will be apt to catch the vibrations of other minds keyed to the same thought level. On the other hand, if we get into the habit of thinking thoughts of a lower character, we will soon be echoing the low order of thought emanating from the minds of the thousands thinking along the same lower lines.

We are largely what we have thought ourselves into being, the balance being represented by the type or level of the suggestions and thought of others, which have reached us either directly by verbal suggestions or telepathically by means of such thought-waves. Our general mental attitude, however, determines the type or level of the thought-waves received from others as well as the thoughts emanating from ourselves. We receive only such thoughts as those that are in harmony with the general mental attitude held by ourselves; the thoughts not in harmony affecting us very little, as they awaken no response in us.

The person who believes thoroughly in themself and maintains a positive strong mental attitude of Confidence and Determination is not likely to be affected by the adverse and negative thoughts of Discouragement and Failure emanating from the minds of other persons in whom these last qualities predominate. At the same time these negative thoughts, if they reach one whose mental attitude is pitched on a low key, deepen their negative state and add fuel to the fire which is consuming their strength, or, if you prefer this figure, serve to further smother the fire of their energy and activity.

We attract to us the thoughts of others who are on the same level of thought.

We attract to us the thoughts of others who are on the same level of thought. The one who thinks at the vibration of success will then be in tune with the minds of others thinking at the same vibration. They will help the person, and they will help them. The one who allows their mind to dwell constantly upon thoughts of failure brings themself into close touch with the minds of other "failure" people, and each will tend to pull the other down even further. The one who thinks that all is evil is apt to see evil everywhere and in everyone, and will be brought into contact with others who will seem to prove their theory. And the one who looks for good in everything and everybody will be likely to attract to themself the experiences and people corresponding to their thought. In other words, we generally see that for which we look.

We generally see that for which we look.

You will be able to carry this idea more clearly if you will think of the Marconi wireless instruments (such as the telegraph and radio), which receive the vibrations only from the sending instrument which has been attuned to the same key, while other telegrams are passing through the air in near vicinity without affecting the instrument. The same law applies to the operations of thought. We receive the signals that only corresponds to our own mental attunement. If we have been discouraged, we may rest assured that we have dropped into a negative level or vibration, and have been affected not only by our own thoughts, but have also received the added depressing thoughts which are constantly being sent out from the minds of others who have not yet learned the law of attraction in the thought world. And if we occasionally rise to heights of enthusiasm and energy, how quickly we feel the inflow of the courageous, daring, energetic, positive thoughts being sent out to others in the world. We recognize this without much trouble when we come in personal contact with people and feel their vibrations, whether depressing or invigorating, as the case may be. But the same law operates when we are not in their presence, although less strongly.

The mind has many degrees, or levels, ranging from the highest positive note to the lowest negative note, with many notes in between, varying in level according to their respective distance from the positive or negative extreme.

When your mind is operating along positive lines you feel strong, buoyant, bright, cheerful, happy, confident, and courageous, and are enabled to do your work well, to carry out your intentions, and progress on your road to Success. You send out strong positive thought, which affects others and causes them to co-operate with you or to follow your lead, according to their own mental keynote.

When you are playing on the extreme negative end of the

mental spectrum you feel depressed, weak, passive, dull, fearful. You might find yourself unable to make progress or to succeed, and your effect upon others is practically *nil*. You follow rather than lead others, and might even be used as a human doormat by some who appear more positive.

In some people the positive element seems to predominate, and in others the negative quality seems to be more in evidence. There are, of course, widely varying degrees of positiveness and negativeness, and B may be negative to A, while positive to C. When two people first meet there is generally a silent mental conflict in which their respective minds test their quality of positiveness, and fix their relative position toward each other. This process may be unconscious in many cases, but it occurs nevertheless. The adjustment is often automatic, but occasionally the struggle is so sharp—the persons being so well matched—that the matter forces itself into the consciousness of the two people. Sometimes both parties are so much alike in their degrees of positiveness that they practically fail to come to terms, mentally; they never really are able to get along with each other, and they are either mutually repelled and separate, or else they stay together amid constant broils and wrangling.

We are either positive or negative to everyone with whom we come into contact. We may be positive to our children, our employees, and dependents, but we are at the same time negative to others.

Of course, something may occur and we will suddenly become more positive than the person to whom we have heretofore been negative. We frequently see cases of this kind. And as the knowledge of these mental laws becomes more well-known we will see many more instances of people asserting themselves and making use of their new-found power.

You possess the power to raise the vibration of your mind to a positive level whenever you choose.

But remember, you possess the power to raise the vibration of your mind to a positive level whenever you choose. And, of course, it is equally true that you may allow yourself to drop to a low, negative level by carelessness or a weak will.

There are more people on the negative plane of thought than on the positive plane, and consequently there are more negative thought vibrations in operation in our mental atmosphere.

There are more people on the negative plane of thought than on the positive plane, and consequently there are more negative thought vibrations in operation in our mental atmosphere. But, happily for us, this is counterbalanced by the fact that a positive thought is infinitely more powerful than a negative one. If we choose, we can raise ourselves to a higher mental key and we can shut out the depressing thoughts, and may increase the vibrations corresponding with our changed mental attitude. This is one of the secrets of the affirmations and auto-suggestions used by the several schools of Mental Science and other New Thought spiritual centers. There is no particular merit in affirmations of themselves, but they serve a two-fold purpose: (1) They tend to establish new mental attitudes within us and act wonderfully in the direction of character building—the science of making ourselves over. (2) They tend to raise our mental vibration so that we may get the benefit of the positive thought-waves of others on the same plane of thought.

Whether or not we believe in them, we are constantly making affirmations. The person who asserts that they can and will do a thing—and asserts it earnestly—develops in themself the qualities conducive to the well doing of that thing, and at the same time places their mind in the proper vibration to receive all the thought-waves likely to help them in the doing. If, on the other hand, one says and feels that they are going to fail, they will smother the thoughts coming from their own subconscious mentality which are intended to help them, and at the same time will place themself in tune with the Failure-thought of the world—and there is plenty of the latter kind of thought around, I can tell you.

> **Do not allow yourselves to be affected by the adverse and negative thoughts of those around you.**

Do not allow yourselves to be affected by the adverse and negative thoughts of those around you. Rise to the upper chambers of your mental dwelling, and key yourself up to a strong level, away above the vibrations on the lower planes of thought. Then you will not only be immune to their negative vibrations but will be in touch with the great body of strong positive thought coming from those of your own plane of development.

My aim will be to direct and train you in the proper use

of thought and will, that you may have yourself well in hand and may be able to strike the positive key, or vibration, at any moment you may feel it necessary. It is not necessary to strike the extreme note on all occasions. The better plan is to keep yourself in a comfortable level without much strain, and to have the means at command whereby you can raise the level at once when an occasion demands. By this knowledge you will not be at the mercy of the old automatic action of the mind, but may have it well under your own control.

> *Development of the will is very much like the development of a muscle—a matter of practice and gradual improvement. At first it is apt to be challenging, but with each trial one grows stronger until the new strength becomes real and permanent.*

Development of the will is very much like the development of a muscle—a matter of practice and gradual improvement. At first it is apt to be challenging, but with each trial one grows stronger until the new strength becomes real and permanent. Many of us have made ourselves positive under sudden calls or emergencies. We are in the habit of "bracing up" when occasion demands. But by intelligent practice you will become so strengthened that your habitual state will be equal to your "bracing up" stage now. Then when you find it necessary due to another challenge, you will be able to reach a new stage not dreamed of at present.

I am not advocating that you live in a state of high tension continuously. This is not at all desirable, because it is apt to be too much of a strain upon you. It is better to be able to relax and assume a certain degree of receptiveness, knowing that you are always able to spring back to the more active state at will. The habitually active person loses much enjoyment and recreation. You need both active and receptive periods of time, both can be positive. Active, you give out energy; receptive, you take in energy. Positive, you are a teacher; receptive, a student. It is not only a good thing to be a good teacher, but it is also very important to be a good listener at times.

3

A TALK ABOUT THE MIND

||||||||||||||||||||||||||||||||||||||||||||||||||

We have but one mind, but that mind has many mental faculties, or abilities. Each faculty is capable of functioning along two different lines of mental effort. There are no distinct dividing lines separating the two several functions of a faculty, but they shade into each other as do the colors of the spectrum.

For example, an Active effort of any faculty of the mind is the result of a direct impulse imparted at the time of the effort. A Passive effort of any faculty of the mind is the result of either a preceding Active effort of the same mind; an Active effort of another along the lines of suggestion; Thought Vibrations from the mind of another; Thought impulses from an ancestor, transmitted by the laws of heredity (including impulses transmitted from generation to generation from the time of the original vibratory impulse imparted by the Primal Cause—which impulses gradually unfold when the proper state of evolutionary development is reached).

The Active effort is new-born—freshly made in the moment, while the Passive effort is from memory and history, and, in fact, is often the result of vibratory impulses imparted in ages long past. The Active effort makes its own way, brushing aside the impeding vines and kicking from its path the obstructing stones. The Passive effort travels along the beaten path.

A new thought or action, originally caused by an Active effort of faculty, may become automatic by continued repetition, or habit. How? By the repeated Active effort, which develops into a strong momentum and carries it forward. There it continues, until it is stopped by another Active effort.

Thoughts or actions, which have continued along Passive lines may be ended or corrected by an Active, or conscious, effort. The Active function creates, changes, or finishes. The Passive function carries on the work given it by the Active function and obeys orders and suggestions.

The Active function produces the thought-habit, or motion-habit, and imparts to it the vibrations which carry it on along the Passive lines thereafter. In other words, the new thought or action becomes passive, or automatic, once we stay with it long enough. The Active function also has the power to send forth vibrations which neutralize the momentum of the thought-habit, or motion-habit; it also is able to launch a *new* thought-habit, or motion-habit, with stronger vibrations, which overcomes and absorbs the first thought, or motion, and substitutes the new one.

All thought-impulses, or motion-impulses, once started, will then continue to vibrate along passive, automatic lines until changed or ended by subsequent impulses imparted by the Active function, or other controlling power. The continuance of the original impulse adds momentum and force to it, and renders its change or dissolution more difficult. This explains that which is called "the force of habit." I think that this will be readily understood by those who have struggled to overcome a habit which had been easily acquired. This Law of Attraction applies to good habits as well as bad. The lesson is clear.

Several of the faculties of the mind often combine to produce a single manifestation. A task to be performed may call for the combined exercise of several faculties, some of which may manifest by Active effort and others by Passive effort together.

When you are met with new conditions—new problems or situations—it calls for the exercise of Active, conscious effort; while a familiar problem, or task, can be easily handled by the Passive effort without the assistance of Active effort.

There is in Nature an instinctive tendency of living organisms to perform certain actions, the tendency of an organized body to seek that which satisfies the wants of its organism. This tendency is sometimes called Appetency, meaning a strong desire or propensity. It is really a Passive mental impulse, originating with the impetus imparted by the Primal Cause, and transmitted along the lines of evolutionary development, gaining strength and power as it progresses. The impulse of the Primal Cause is assisted by the powerful upward attraction exerted by the Absolute.

In plant life this tendency is plainly discernible, ranging from the lesser exhibitions in the lower types to the greater in the higher types. It is that which is generally spoken of as the "life force" in plants. It is, however, a manifestation of rudimentary mentation, or mental activity, functioning along the lines of Passive effort. In some of the higher forms of plant life there appears a faint color of independent "life action"—a faint indication of choice of volition. Writers on plant life relate many remarkable instances of this phenomenon. It is, undoubtedly, an exhibition of rudimentary Active mentation.

In the lower animal kingdom a very high degree of Passive mental effort is found. And, varying in degree in the several families and species, a considerable amount of Active mentation is apparent. The lower animal undoubtedly possesses Reason seemingly in a lesser degree than humans, and, in fact, the display of volitional mentation exhibited by an intelligent animal is often nearly as high as that shown by a young child or more.

As a child, before birth, shows in its body the stages of the physical evolution of humans, so does a child, before and after birth—until maturity—manifest the stages of the *mental* evolution of humans.

Humans, perhaps the highest type of life yet produced, at least upon this planet, shows the highest form of Passive mentation, and also a much higher development of Active mentation than is seen in animals, and yet the degrees of that power seem to vary widely among us. These degrees are not dependent upon the amount of "culture," social position, or education possessed by the individual. Mental Culture and Mental Development are two very different things.

You have but to look around you to see the different stages

of the development of Active mentation, or process of reasoning and thinking, in people. The reasoning of many is scarcely more than Passive mentation, exhibiting but little of the qualities of volitional, conscious thought. They prefer to let others think for them. Active mentation, or decision and thinking, tires them, and they find the instinctive, automatic, Passive mental process much easier. Their minds work along the lines of least resistance. They are but little more than human sheep.

Science seems to show that as the lower forms of life progressed in the evolutionary scale, they developed new faculties, which were latent within them. These faculties always manifested in the form of rudimentary Passive functioning, and afterwards worked up, through higher Passive forms, until the Active functions were brought into play. The evolutionary process still continues, the invariable tendency being toward the goal of highly developed Active mentation. This evolutionary progress is caused by the vibratory impulse imparted by the Primal Cause, aided by the uplifting attraction of the Absolute.

This law of evolution is still in progress, and we are beginning to develop new powers of mind, which are first manifesting themselves along the lines of Passive effort. Some have developed these new faculties to a considerable degree, and it is possible that before long they will be able to exercise them along the line of their Active functions. In fact, this power has already been attained by a few.

The receptiveness of the mind to new conscious choices, or the Will, can be increased by properly directed practice. That which we are in the habit of referring to as the "strengthening of the Will" is in reality the training of the mind to recognize and absorb the Power Within. The Will is strong enough; it does not need strengthening, but the mind needs to be trained to receive and act upon the suggestions of the Will. The Will is the outward manifestation of the I AM, the Absolute within us. The Will current is flowing in full strength along the spiritual wires; but you must learn how to use it before it works for you. This is a somewhat different idea from that which you have been in the habit of receiving from writers on the subject of Will Power, but it is correct, as you will demonstrate to your own satisfaction if you will follow up the subject by experiments along the proper lines.

The pull of the Absolute draws us upward, and the vibratory force of the Primal Impulse has not yet exhausted itself. The time of evolutionary development has come when we can help ourself. The one who understands the Law can accomplish wonders by means of the development of the powers of the mind; while the one who turns their back upon the truth will suffer from their lack of knowledge of the Law.

One who understands the laws of their mental being, develops their latent powers and uses them intelligently. They do not despise their own Passive mental functions, but rather makes good use of them. They charge the Passive, subconscious mind with the duties for which it is best fitted, and is able to obtain wonderful results from their work, having mastered them and trained them to do the bidding of the Higher Self. When the Passive, or subconscious mind, fails to do their work properly they can regulate them, and their knowledge prevents them from meddling with the subconscious unintelligently or recklessly, and thereby doing themself harm. They develop the faculties and powers latent within them and learn how to manifest them along the line of Active choice and decision in addition to the Passive. They have come to realize that both Active and Passive functions of the Mind are but tools. They have banished Fear, and enjoy Freedom. They have found *themself.* In short, they have learned the secret of that Divine within, the place of the I AM.

4

MIND BUILDING

||||||||||||||||||||||||||||||||||||||||||||||

We can build up our mind and make it what we choose or will. In fact, we are mind building every hour of our lives, either consciously or unconsciously. The majority of us are doing the work unconsciously, but those who have seen a little below the surface of things have taken the matter in hand and have become conscious creators of their own mentality. They are no longer subject to the suggestions and influences of others but have become masters of themselves. They assert the "I," and require compliance from the subordinate mental faculties. In other words, conscious choices and decisions, or the "I," will in turn activate our subconscious mind. The "I" is the sovereign of the mind, and what we call WILL is the instrument of the "I." Of course, there is something back of this, and the Universal Will is higher than the Will of the Individual, but the latter is in much closer touch with the Universal Will than is generally supposed. When one conquers the lower self, and asserts the "I," they become in close touch with the Universal Will and partakes largely of its wonderful power. The moment one asserts the "I," and "finds themself," they establish a close connection between the Individual Will and the Universal Will. But before they are able to avail themself of the mighty power at their command, they must first effect the proficiency of the lower self, or the subconscious.

Think of the illogicality of one claiming to manifest what they want, when they don't assert their Active mind, and instead are only Passive in life. They are at the mercy of their own subconscious, which should be subordinate. Or the one who believes they are powerless to their moods, addictions, and even fate, and, at the same time, tries to claim the benefits of the Will.

I am speaking of Self-Mastery—the assertion of the "I" over the subordinate parts of oneself. In the higher view of the subject, this "I" is the only *real* Self, and the rest is the non-self; but in this book we will use the word "self" as meaning the entire human. Before one can assert the "I" in its full strength they must obtain the complete mastery of the subordinate parts of the self. All things are good when we learn to master them, but no thing is good when it masters us. Just so long as we allow the lower portions of the self to give us orders, we feel powerless. It is only when the "I" mounts to the throne and lifts the scepter that order is established and things assume their proper relation to each other.

To be clear, we are finding no fault with those who are swayed by their lower selves—they have not yet learned how to use the Law of Attraction , and hopefully will work up to it in time. But we are calling the attention of those who are ready, to the fact that the conscious mind can now assert its will, and that the subjective mind must obey. Orders must be given and carried out. The time to do it is Now.

You might have been Passive in your life up to now. You have been allowing the mental kingdom to be misgoverned by the subconscious. You have believed yourself to be powerless against moods, emotions, thoughts of unworthiness, and negativity. It is time to re-establish order in your mental kingdom.

You are able to assert mastery over any emotion, appetite, passion, or class of thoughts by the assertion of your Will. You can order fear to go to the rear; jealousy to leave your presence; hate to depart from your sight; anger to hide itself; worry to cease troubling you; uncontrolled desires to bow in submission and to become humble followers instead of leaders—all by the assertion of your "I." You may surround yourself with the glorious company of Courage, Love, and Self-Control, by the same means. You may put down the rebellion and secure peace and order in your mental kingdom if you will only utter the mandate and insist upon its implementation. Before you can gain what you want, you must establish the proper internal conditions—and must show your ability to govern your own mental kingdom. The first battle is the conquest of the lesser self by the Real Self.

AFFIRMATION

I Am Asserting the Mastery of My Real Self

But be sure to back up the words with the thought and feelings inspiring them, and do not merely repeat them parrot-like.

Repeat these words *earnestly* and positively during the day, at least once an hour, and particularly when you are confronted with conditions which tempt you to act on the lines of the lesser, passive, more limited self instead of following the course dictated by the Real Self. In the moment of doubt and hesitation, say these words earnestly, and your way will be made clear to you. Repeat them several times after you retire and settle yourself to sleep. But be sure to back up the words with the thought and feelings inspiring them, and do not merely repeat them parrot-like. Form the mental image of the Real Self asserting its mastery over the subconscious planes of your mind—see your conscious thought in control of your subconscious. When you do, you will become conscious of an influx of new thoughts and ideas, and things which have seemed hard for you will suddenly become much easier. You will feel that you have yourself well in hand, and that YOU are the leader of your own life and not the follower. The thought you are holding will manifest itself in action, and you will steadily grow to become that which you have in mind. This is how to activate the Law of Attraction in your own life.

EXERCISE

Stay focused on the thoughts and actions which align with what you desire, rather than fall back into the thoughts and habits of what keeps you from what you desire. For example, when you are tempted to burst into anger—instead choose to respond in a way that matches what you really want, and you will experience more power in that moment. Some emotions, like unwarranted or uncontrolled anger, are not worthy of the developed Self. When you feel annoyed and cross, remember who and what you are—you are made from The Absolute—and rise above your feeling, which is temporary. When you feel fearful, remember that the Real Self fears nothing, and draw on that courage. When you feel jealousy inciting, think of your higher nature, and laugh. And so on, asserting the Real Self and not allowing the things on the lower plane of mentality to disturb you. They are unworthy of you, and must be taught to keep their places. Do not allow these things to master you—they should be your subjects, not your masters. You must get away from this reactive plane, and the only way to do so is to cut loose from these phases of thought which have been "running things" in your life, only to suit themselves. You may have trouble at the start of controlling your mind and emotions, but keep at it and you will have that satisfaction which comes only from conquering those parts of your nature. You have been passive in your own life long enough—now is the time to lead yourself. If you will follow these exercises faithfully you will be a different being in a short time, and will look back with a smile to your former condition. But it takes work. Will YOU make the effort?

5

THE SECRET OF THE WILL

IIIIIIIIIIIIIIIIIIIIIIIIIIIIIIIIIIIIIIIIIIIIIIIIIII

While psychologists may differ in their theories regarding the nature of the Will, none deny its existence, nor question its power. All persons recognize the power of strong Will, and all can see how it may be used to overcome the greatest obstacles. But few realize that the Will may be developed and strengthened by intelligent, consistent practice. They feel that they could accomplish wonders if they had a strong Will, but instead of attempting to develop a strong Will, they content themselves with regrets. They sigh, but do nothing.

Those who have investigated the subject closely know that Will Power, with all its latent possibilities and mighty powers, may be developed, disciplined, controlled, and directed, just as may be any other of Nature's forces. It does not matter what theory you may entertain about the nature of the Will, you will obtain the results if you practice intelligently.

Personally, I have a somewhat odd theory about the Will.

I believe that everyone has, potentially, a strong Will, and that all we have to do is to train our mind to make use of it. I think that in the higher regions of everyone's mind is a great supply of Will Power awaiting our use. The Will current is running along the mental wires, and all that it is necessary to do is to raise the mental vibration and connect with the power for your use. The supply is unlimited, for your little storage battery is connected with the great power house of the Universal Will Power, and the power is inexhaustible. Your Will does not need training—but your Mind does. The mind is the instrument, and the supply of Will Power is proportionate to the quality of the instrument through which it manifests. But you needn't accept this theory if you don't like it. This lesson will fit your theory as well as mine.

Your Will does not need training—but your Mind does.

The one who has developed their mind so that it will allow the Will Power of what they desire to manifest through it has opened up wonderful possibilities for themself. Not only have they found a great power at their command, but they are able to bring into play and use the faculties, talents, and abilities beyond what they have dreamed of. This secret of the Will is the magic key which opens all doors.

Many of us feel that if we would but exert our Will, we might accomplish wonders. But somehow we do not seem to want to take the trouble—at any rate, we do not get to the actual willing point of action. We put it off from time to time, and talk vaguely of "someday," but that someday never comes.

We instinctively feel the power of the Will, but we haven't enough energy to exercise it, and so drift along with the tide, unless perhaps some friendly difficulty arises, some helpful obstacle appears in our path, or some kindly pain stirs us into action, in either of which cases we are compelled to assert our Will and thus begin to accomplish something.

The trouble in these instances is that we do not want our desire strong enough to make us exert our Will Power. *We don't want to hard enough.* We might have fallen into mental laziness and have chosen a weak desire. If you do not like the word "desire" substitute for it the word "aspiration." (Some people call the lower impulses desires, and the higher, aspirations—it's all a matter of words, take your choice.) That is the trouble. Let someone be in danger of losing their life—or let someone be in danger of losing a great love—and you will witness a startling exhibition of Will Power from an unexpected source. Let a parent's child be threatened with danger, and the parent will manifest a degree of Courage and Will that sweeps all before it. And yet the same person might normally be passive, and not able to do even easy actions toward their aspirations. A child will do all sorts of work if they consider it play, and yet the same child can scarcely force themself to do their homework or chores. Strong Will follows strong Desire. If you really want to do a thing very much, you can usually develop the Will Power to accomplish it.

Strong Will follows strong Desire. If you really want to do a thing very much, you can usually develop the Will Power to accomplish it.

The trouble is that you have not really *wanted* to do these things, and yet you blame your Will. You say that you *do* want to do it, but if you stop to think you will see that you really want to do something else more than the thing in question. *You are not willing to pay the price of attainment.* Stop a moment and analyze this statement and apply it to your own case.

You, like most people, are mentally lazy—that's the trouble. Don't talk to me about not having enough Will. You have a great storehouse of Will awaiting your use, but you have chosen not to use it. Now, if you are really serious about improving things, get to work and first find out what you really want to do—then start to work and *do* it. Never mind about the Will Power—you'll find there is always a full supply of that whenever you need it. The thing to do is to get to the point where you will *resolve* to Will. That's the real test—*the resolving*. Think of these things a little, and make up your mind whether or not you seriously want to be figure out a new life experience enough to work on it consistently and earnestly.

Many excellent essays and books have been written on this subject, all of which agree regarding the greatness of Will Power, and they will use the most enthusiastic terms; but few have anything to say about how this power may be acquired by those who do not yet have it, or who possess it in but a limited degree. Some of these books have given exercises designed to "strengthen" the Will, which really strengthens the Mind so that it is able to draw upon the Will's store of power. But they have generally overlooked the secret to developing the mind so that it may become the efficient instrument of the Will. The secret is this: Auto-Suggestion.

AUTO-SUGGESTION

I Am Using My Will Power

Say these words several times *earnestly* and positively, immediately after finishing this chapter. Then repeat them frequently during the day, at least once an hour, and particularly when you meet with someone or something that calls for the exercise of Will Power. Also repeat them several times after you retire and settle yourself for sleep. Now, there is nothing in these words unless you back them up with the thought of confident expectation of the result you want. In fact, the thought is "the whole thing," and the words are only pegs upon with which to hang the thought. So think of what you are saying, *and mean what you say.* Don't just say the words, *feel* them. You must use Faith at the start, and again, use the words with a *confident expectation* of the result. Hold the steady thought that you *are* drawing on your storehouse of Will Power, and before long you will find that thought is starting to take form in action, and that your Will Power is manifesting itself. You will feel an influx of strength with each repetition of the words. You will find yourself overcoming difficulties and bad habits, and will be surprised at how things are being smoothed out for you.

EXERCISE

Perform at least *one* disagreeable task each day during the month. If there is any especially disagreeable task which you would like to avoid, *that* is the one for you to perform. It is not given you in order to make you self-sacrificing or anything of that sort—it is given you to *exercise your Will.* Anyone can do a pleasant thing cheerfully, but it takes Will to do the unpleasant thing *cheerfully*; and that is *how* you must do the work. It will prove a most valuable discipline to you. Try it for a month and you will see where it "comes in." If you do not do this exercise you had better stop right here and acknowledge that you do not want Will Power, and are content to stay where you are and perhaps even remain weak and afraid.

6

HOW TO BECOME IMMUNE TO NEGATIVE THOUGHT ATTRACTION

|||||||||||||||||||||||||||||||||||||||||||||||||

The first thing to do to help yourself experience what you desire is to begin to "cut out" fear and worry. Fearful thoughts are the cause of much unhappiness and many failures. You have been told this thing over and over again, but it will bear repeating. Fear is a habit of mind which has been amplified by the negativity of those around us, but from which we may free ourselves through effort and perseverance.

Fear is a habit of mind which has been amplified by the negativity of those around us, but from which we may free ourselves through effort and perseverance.

Strong expectancy is a powerful magnet. The one with strong, confident desires attracts to themselves the things best calculated to help them—persons, things, circumstances, sur-roundings—if they desire them with hope, trust, confidence, and calmness. And, equally true, the one who fears a thing generally manages to start into operation the energy which then can contribute to the thing they feared to become a re-ality. Don't you see, the one who fears really consciously or unconsciously *expects* the feared thing, and, in the eyes of the Law of Attraction, it is the same as if they really *had* wished for or desired it? The Law of Attraction is operative in both cases—the principle is the same. The Law of Attraction works with what you give it—and if you give it fear, that is what it will work with. But if you give it confidence and positivity, then that is what it will work with.

The best way to overcome the habit of fear is to assume the mental attitude of courage, just as the best way to get rid of darkness is to let in the light. It is a waste of time to fight a negative thought-habit by recognizing its force and trying to *deny* it out of existence by mighty efforts. The best, surest, easiest, and quickest method is to instead assume the existence of the positive thought desired in its place; and by constantly dwelling upon the positive thought, manifest it into objective reality.

For example, instead of repeating, "I'm not afraid," say boldly, "I am full of courage," "I am courageous." You must assert, "There's nothing to fear," which, although in the nature of a denial, simply denies the reality of the object causing fear rather than admitting the fear itself and then denying it.

To overcome fear, one should hold firmly to the mental at-titude of courage. We should think courage, say courage, act courage. We should keep the mental picture of courage before us all the time, until it becomes our dominant normal mental attitude. Hold the ideal firmly before you and you will gradually grow to its attainment—the ideal will become manifest.

Let the word "courage" sink deeply into your mind, and then hold it firmly there until the mind fastens it in place. Think of yourself as being courageous—see yourself as acting with courage in trying situations. Feel it. Realize that there is nothing to fear that you cannot handle—that worry and fear usually hinders positive experience rather than help it. Realize that fear paralyzes you, and that courage promotes positive activity. If there is another word that you want to experience rather than courage—freedom, positivity, joy, love, peace, empowered, or others—use that word instead. It's the quality that the word represents that you are looking for.

The person who can confidently, fearlessly, and with expectancy say "I Can and I Will" is a mighty magnet. They will attract just what is needed for their success. On the outside, it will seem like positive things seem to come their way, and people say that person is "lucky." Nonsense! "Luck" has nothing to do with it. It's all in the Mental Attitude. And the Mental Attitude of the "I Can't" or the "I'm Afraid" person directly corresponds to their measure of success. There's no mystery whatsoever about it. It's common sense, but most people don't use it. You have but to look about you to realize the truth of what I have said. Did you ever know a successful person who did not have the "I Can and I Will" thought strong within them? Why, that person will succeed when the "I Can't" person won't, even one who might even have more ability. The first mental attitude brought to the surface dormant, positive qualities within, as well as attracted help from outside; while the second mental attitude not only attracted "I Can't" people and things, but also limited themselves and their own powers from manifesting. I have seen the validity of these views in my own life, and so have many others, and the number of people who *know* these things is growing every day.

> *Let your prevailing thought be "I Can and I Will";*
> *think "I Can and I Will"; dream "I Can and I Will";*
> *say "I Can and I Will"; act "I Can and I Will."*

Don't waste the power of your Thoughts, but use them to your advantage. Remember, our thoughts attract and put us in the path of what we are thinking about. That is the Law of Attraction. Therefore, stop attracting to yourself failure, unhappiness, negativity, sorrow—begin now and send out a current of bright, positive, happy thought. Let your prevailing thought be "I Can and I Will"; *think* "I Can and I Will"; *dream* "I Can and I Will"; *say* "I Can and I Will"; *act* "I Can and I Will." Live on the "I Can and I Will" plane of vibration, and before you are aware of it, you will feel the new vibrations manifesting themselves in action; you will see them bring results; you will be conscious of the new point of view; you will realize that your own is coming to you. When "I Can and I Will" is your compass, you will feel better, act better, see better, feel better, and BE better in every way.

Fear is the parent of worry, hate, jealousy, malice, anger, discontent, failure, and all the rest. The person who rids themself of fear will find that the people and experiences from the vibration of fear have begun to disappear, because that person is now on a different vibration. The only way to be Free is to get rid of fear. Tear it out by the roots. I regard the conquest of fear as the first important step to be taken by those who wish to master the application of Thought Force and the Law of Attraction. So long as fear masters you, you are in no condition to make progress in the realm of Thought, and I strongly suggest that you start to work at once to get rid of this obstruction. You CAN do it—if you only go about it in earnest. And when you have ridded yourself of most of the fears you once held, life will seem entirely different to you—you will feel happier, freer, stronger, more positive, and will be more successful in every undertaking of Life.

Start in today, make up your mind that this intruder must GO—do not compromise matters with fear, but insist upon an absolute surrender on fear's part. You will find the task difficult at first, but each time you oppose fear it will grow weaker, and you will be stronger. Shut off fear's nourishment—starve it to death—it cannot live in a thought-atmosphere of fearlessness. So, start to fill your mind with good, strong, fearless thoughts—keep yourself busy thinking fearlessness, and fear will die of his own accord. Fearlessness is positive—fear is negative, and you may be sure that the positive will prevail.

So long as Fear is around, it fills you with words like "but," "if," "suppose," "I'm afraid," "I can't," "what if," and all the rest, and you will not be able to use your Thought Force to the best advantage. Once you focus on power thoughts to get fear out of the way, you will have clearer sailing, and every inch of thought-sail will catch the wind.

I advise that you start in to do some of the things which you feel you could do if you were not *afraid* to try. Start to work to do these things, affirming "courage" all the way through, and you will be surprised to see how the changed mental attitude will clear away obstacles from your path, and will make things very much easier than you had anticipated. Exercises of this kind will develop you wonderfully, and you will be much gratified at the result of a little practice along these lines.

There are many things before you which are awaiting to be accomplished, which you can master if you will only throw aside the yoke of fear—if you will only refuse to accept the negativity of those around you, and will boldly assert the "I" and its power. And the best way to vanquish fear is to assert "courage" and stop thinking of fear. By this plan you will train the mind into new habits of thought, thus eradicating the old negative thoughts which have been pulling you down, and holding you back. Take the word "courage" with you as your watchword and manifest it in action. The only thing to fear is fear itself.

7

THE TRANSMUTATION OF NEGATIVE THOUGHT

||||||||||||||||||||||||||||||||||||||||||||||||||||

Worry is the child of fear—if you kill out fear, worry will die for want of nourishment. This advice is very old, and yet it is always worthy of repetition, for it is a lesson of which we are greatly in need. Some people think that if we kill out fear and worry we will never be able to accomplish anything. I have read editorials in the great journals in which the writers held that without worry one can never accomplish any of the great tasks of life, because worry is necessary to stimulate interest and work. This is nonsense, no matter who utters it. Worry never helped one to accomplish anything; on the contrary, it stands in the way of accomplishment and attainment.

Worry never helped one to accomplish anything; on the contrary, it stands in the way of accomplishment and attainment.

The motive underlying action and "doing things" is desire and interest. If you earnestly desire a thing, you naturally become very much interested in its accomplishment, and are quick to seize upon anything likely to help you to gain the thing you wants. More than that, your mind starts up a work on the subconscious plane that brings into the field of consciousness many ideas of value and importance. Desire and interest are the causes that result in success. Worry is not desire. It is true that if one's surroundings and environments become intolerable, they are driven in desperation to some efforts that will result in throwing off the undesirable conditions and in the acquiring of those more in harmony with their desire. But this is only another form of desire—the person who desires something different from what they have; and when their desire becomes strong enough that their entire interest is given to the task, they make a mighty effort, and the change is accomplished. But it wasn't worry that caused the effort. Worry could content itself with wringing its hands and moaning "Woe is me," and wearing its nerves to a frazzle, and accomplishing nothing. Desire acts differently. It grows stronger as our conditions become intolerable, and finally when we feel the hurt so strongly that we can't stand it any longer, that is when we will say, "I *won't* stand this any longer—I *will* make a change," and lo! then desire springs into action. We keep on "wanting" a change the worst way (worst meaning most urgent, which is the *best* way) and our interest and attention being given to the task of deliverance, we begin to make things move. Worry never accomplished anything. Worry is negative and death producing. Desire and ambition are positive and life producing. A person may worry himself to death and yet nothing will be accomplished, but let that same person transmute their worry and discontent into desire and interest, coupled with a belief that they are able to make the change—the "I Can and I Will" idea—then something happens. The Law of Attraction is now set toward the positive rather than the negative.

> *Thoughts will come to you from the great reserve stock in your mind and you will start to manifest them in action.*

Yes, fear and worry must go before we can do much. One must proceed to cast out these negative intruders and replace them with confidence and hope. Transmute worry into strong desire. Then you will find that your interest is awakened and you will begin to think things of interest to you. Thoughts will come to you from the great reserve stock in your mind and you will start to manifest them in action. Moreover you will be placing yourself in harmony with similar thoughts of others, and will draw to you aid and assistance from the great volume of thought-waves with which the world is filled. You draw to yourself the thought-waves that correspond in character with the nature of the prevailing thoughts in your own mind—your mental attitude. That is how you begin to set into motion the great Law of Attraction, whereby you draw to yourself people and situations that are likely to help you. This Law of Attraction is not a joke, it is not a metaphysical absurdity. It is a great live working principle of Nature, as anyone may learn by experimenting and observing it for themself.

To succeed in anything you must want it very much— desire must be in evidence in order to attract. If you have weak desires you will attract very little to yourself. The stronger the desire the greater the force set into motion. You must want a thing hard enough before you can get it. You must want it more than you do the things around you, and you must be prepared to pay the price for it. The price is letting go of certain lesser desires that stand in the way of the accomplishment of the greater one. Comfort, ease, leisure, amusements, and many other things may have to go (not always, though). It all depends on what you want, not in the short term, but you must have long-term vision. As a rule, the greater the thing desired, the greater the price to be paid for it. Nature believes in adequate compensation. But if you really desire a thing in earnest, you will pay the price without question; for the desire will overpower the importance of the other things.

You say that you want a thing very much, and are doing everything possible toward its attainment? Pshaw! You are only playing with a faint desire. Do you want the thing as much as a prisoner wants freedom? Look at the almost miraculous things accomplished by prisoners desiring freedom. Look how they work through steel plates and stone walls using only a bit of stone. Is your desire as strong as that? Do you work for the desired thing as if your life depended upon it? If you don't, then you don't know what desire is. I tell you if you want a thing as much as the prisoner wants freedom, or as much as a strongly vital person wants life, then you will be able to sweep away obstacles and impediments apparently immovable. And something inside you knows that this is true. The key to attainment is made up of desire, confidence, and will. This key will open many doors.

Fear paralyzes desire—it scares the life out of it. You must get rid of fear. There have been times in my life when Fear would get hold of me and take a good, firm grip on my vitals, and I would lose all hope; all interest; all ambition; all desire. But, thank goodness, I have always managed to throw off the grip of the monster and face my difficulty head on; and lo! things would seem to be straightened out for me in some way or another. Either the difficulty would melt away, or I would be given means to overcome it, or get around it, or under or over it. It is strange how this works, and I could never predict how it would happen. No matter how great is the difficulty, when we finally face it with courage and confidence in ourselves, we seem to pull through somehow, and then we can look back and wonder what we were scared about. This is not a mere fancy, it is the working of the mighty Law of Attraction, which we do not as yet fully understand, but which we may prove at any time.

People often ask: "It's all very well for you to say 'Don't worry,' but what's a person to do when they think of all the possible things ahead of them, which might upset them and their plans?" Well, all that I can say is that the person who is foolish to bother about thinking of troubles to come at some time in the future is inviting troubles to come. The majority of things that we worry about don't come to pass at all; a large proportion of the others come in a milder form than we had anticipated, and there are always other things and people which come at the same time which help us to overcome the trouble, especially if we are thinking positively. The future holds in store for us not only difficulties to be overcome, but also avenues to help us in overcoming the difficulties. Things adjust themselves. Look back at what seemed like trouble you went through, and do you not see that they were all worked out in some way or another, often to your benefit? When and if challenges come in the future, you will somehow find yourself able to meet it.

It has been well said that nine-tenths of the worries are over things which never come to pass, and that the other tenth is over things of little or no account. So what's the use in using up all your reserve force in fretting over future troubles, if this be so? Better wait until your troubles really come before you worry. You will find that by this storing up of energy you will be able to meet about any sort of trouble that comes your way.

What is it that uses up all the energy in the average person, anyway? Is it the real overcoming of difficulties, or is it the worrying about impending troubles? I think it's the latter. It's always "Tomorrow, tomorrow," and yet tomorrow never comes just as we feared it would. Tomorrow is all right; it carries in its grip good things as well as troubles. Bless my soul, when I sit down and think over the things which I once feared might possibly descend upon me, I laugh! Where are those feared things now? I don't know—have almost forgotten that I ever feared them. And by staying in the lane of the positive, I create a more positive future. That doesn't mean challenges don't come, but I've learned to view the challenges as opportunities.

You do not need to *fight* worry—that isn't the way to overcome the habit. Just practice concentration, and then learn to concentrate upon something right before you, and you will find that the worry thought has vanished. The mind can think of but one thing at a time, and if you concentrate upon a constructive thing, the negative thing will fade away. There are better ways of overcoming objectionable thoughts than by fighting them. Learn to concentrate upon thoughts of an opposite character, and you will have solved the problem. You will be using the Law of Attraction.

The mind can think of but one thing at a time, and if you concentrate upon a constructive thing, the negative thing will fade away.

When the mind is full of worry thoughts, it cannot find time to work out plans to benefit you.

There's no sense in worrying; nothing has ever been gained by it, and nothing ever will be.

But when you have concentrated upon bright, helpful, positive thoughts, you will discover that it will start to work subconsciously; and when the time comes you will find all sorts of plans and methods by which you will be able to meet the demands upon you. Keep your mental attitude right, and all things will be added unto you. There's no sense in worrying; nothing has ever been gained by it, and nothing ever will be. Bright, cheerful, and happy thoughts *attract* bright, cheerful, and happy things to us—worry drives them away. Cultivate the right mental attitude.

8

THE LAW OF MENTAL CONTROL

||||||||||||||||||||||||||||||||||||||||||||

Your thoughts are either faithful servants or tyrannical masters—just as you allow them to be. The decision is with you; take your choice. They will either go about your work under direction of the firm will, doing it the best they know how, not only in your waking hours, but when you are asleep—some of our best mental work being performed for us when our conscious mentality is at rest, as is evidenced by the fact that when the morning comes we find troublesome problems have been worked out for us during the night, after we had dismissed them from our minds—apparently; or they will ride all over us and make us their followers if we are foolish enough to allow them to do so. More than half the people of the world are powerless to every wandering thought which may see fit to torment them.

Your mind was given to you for your good, and for your own use—not to use you. There are very few people who seem to realize this and who understand the art of managing the mind. The key to the mystery is concentration. A little practice will help to develop within you the power to use your mental machine more effectively. When you have some mental work to do concentrate upon it to the exclusion of everything else, and you will find that the mind will get right down to business—to the work at hand—and matters will be cleared up in no time. There is an absence of friction, and all wasted motion or lost power is obviated. Every pound of energy is put to use, and every revolution of the mental driving-wheel counts for something. It pays to be able to be a competent mental engineer.

And the one who understands how to run their mental engine knows that one of the important things is to be able to stop it when the work has been done. That person docs not keep putting coal in the furnace, and maintaining a high pressure after the work is finished, or when the day's portion of the work has been done, and the fires should be banked until the next day. Some people act as if the engine should be kept running whether there was any work to be done or not, and then they complain if they feel worn out and drained of energy. These mental engines are fine machines, and need intelligent care.

> *The best way to move your mind from worry is to think of something else—as far different from the obtruding thought as possible.*

To those who are acquainted with the laws of mental control it seems absurd for one to lie awake at night fretting about the problems of the day that was, or more often, of tomorrow. It is just as easy to slow down the mind as it is to slow down an engine, and many people are learning to do this these days. The best way to move your mind from worry is to think of something else—as far different from the obtruding thought as possible. There is no use fighting an objectionable thought with the purpose of "defeating" it; that is a great waste of energy, and the more you keep on saying, "I won't think of this thing!" the more it keeps on coming into your mind, for you are holding it there for the purpose of defeating it. Let it go; don't give it another thought. Instead, fix your mind on something entirely different, and keep the attention there by a little effort. A little practice will do much for you in this direction. There is only room for one thing at a time in the focus of attention; so put all your attention upon one thought, and the others will sneak off. Try it for yourself.

9

ASSERTING THE LIFE FORCE

have spoken to you of the advantage of getting rid of Fear. Now I wish to put LIFE into you. Many of you have been going along as if you were dead—no ambition—no energy—no vitality—no interest—no life. This will never do. You feel like you are stagnating. It's time to wake up and display a few signs of life! This world is not the place in which you can stalk around like a living corpse—this is the place for wide-awake, active, *alive* people, and a good general awakening is what is needed. Sometimes I think it would take nothing less than a blast from Gabriel's trumpet to awaken some of the people who are stalking around thinking that they are alive but who are really dead to all that makes life worthwhile.

We must let Life flow through us and allow it to express itself naturally. Do not let the little worries of life, or the big ones either, depress you and cause you to lose your vitality.

We must let Life flow through us and allow it to express itself naturally. Do not let the little worries of life, or the big ones either, depress you and cause you to lose your vitality. Assert the Life Force within you, and manifest it in every thought, act and deed, and before long you will be exhilarated and fairly bubbling over with vitality and energy.

Put a little energy into your work—into your pleasures—into yourself. Stop doing things in a half-hearted way, and begin to take an interest in what you are doing, saying, and thinking. Have you noticed that when you give half-hearted effort you seem to get half-hearted results? It is astonishing how much interest we may find in the ordinary things of life, if we will only wake up. There are interesting things all around us—interesting events occurring every moment—but we will not be aware of them unless we assert our life force and begin to actually live instead of merely existing.

No one ever amounted to anything unless they put life, and interest, and curiosity into the tasks of everyday life—the acts—the thoughts. What the world needs is people who are *alive*. Just look into the eyes of the people whom you meet and see how few of them are really *alive*. Most of them lack that expression of conscious life which distinguishes the one who *lives* from the one who simply *exists*.

I want you to acquire this sense of conscious life so that you may manifest it in your life and show what raising your thoughts to the vibration of positivity has done for you. I want you to get to work today and choose to see the good in as many people and experiences as possible, especially those that are hardest to see the good in. Be curious, see problems as puzzles to be solved. You can do this if you will only take the proper interest in the task.

AFFIRMATION AND EXERCISE

I Am Alive

Fix in your mind the thought that the "I" within you is very much alive and that you are manifesting life fully, both mentally and physically. And keep this thought there, aiding yourself with constant repetitions of the watchword. Don't let the thought escape you, but when other thoughts come into your mind, keep refocusing on "I Am Alive." Keep it before your mental vision as much as possible. Repeat the watchword when you wake up in the morning—say it when you retire at night. Say it at meal times, and whenever else you can during the day—at least once an hour. Form the mental picture of yourself as filled with Life and Energy. Live up to it as far as possible. When you start in to perform a task say "I Am Alive" and mix up as much energy and feeling as possible in the task. If you find yourself feeling depressed, say "I Am Alive," and then take a few deep breaths, and with each inhalation let the mind hold the thought that you are breathing in Strength and Life, and as you exhale, hold the thought that you are breathing out all the old, negative conditions and are glad to get rid of them. Then finish up with an earnest, vigorous affirmation: "I Am Alive," and *mean* it when you say it, too.

Let your thoughts take form in action. Don't rest and be content with merely saying that you are alive, but now prove it with your acts. Take an interest in doing things, and don't go around "mooning" or day-dreaming. Get down to business, and LIVE.

10

TRAINING THE HABIT-MIND

||||||||||||||||||||||||||||||||||||||||||||||||||||

Professor William James, the well-known teacher of, and writer upon Psychology, very truly says:

"The great thing in all education is to make our nervous system our ally instead of our enemy. For this we must make automatic and habitual, as early as possible, as many useful actions as we can, and as carefully guard against growing into ways that are likely to be disadvantageous. In the acquisition of a new habit, or the leaving off of an old one, we must take care to launch ourselves with as strong and decided initiative as possible. Never suffer an exception to occur until the new habit is securely rooted in your life. Seize the very first possible opportunity to act on every resolution you make and on every emotional prompting you may experience, in the direction of the habits you aspire to gain."

This advice is along the lines familiar to all students of Mental Science, but it states the matter more plainly than the majority of us have done. It impresses upon us the importance of passing on to the subconscious mind the proper impulses, so that they will become automatic and "second nature." Our subconscious mentality is a great store house for all sorts of suggestions from ourselves and others, and, as it is the "habit-mind," we must be careful to send it the proper material from which it may make habits. If we get into the habit of doing certain things, we may be sure that the subconscious mind will make it easier for us to do just the same thing over and over again, easier each time, until finally we are firmly bound with the ropes and chains of the habit, and find it more or less difficult, sometimes almost impossible, to free ourselves from that thing.

We should cultivate good habits to prepare for an hour of need. The time might come when we will be required to put forth our best efforts, and it rests with us today whether that hour of need shall find us doing the proper thing automatically and almost without thought, or struggling to do it bound down and hindered with the weight of things opposed to that which we desire at that moment.

We must be on guard at all times to prevent the forming of undesirable habits. These are like weeds in our garden. There may be no special harm in doing a certain thing today, or perhaps again tomorrow, but there may be much harm in setting up *the habit* of doing that particular thing. If you are confronted with the question: "Which of these two things should I do?" the best answer is: "I will do the one which I would like to become a habit with me."

In forming a new habit, or in breaking an old one, we should throw ourselves into the task with as much enthusiasm as possible, in order to gain the most ground before the energy expends itself when it meets with friction from the opposing habits already formed. We should start in by making as strong an impression as possible upon the subconscious mentality. Then we should be constantly on guard against temptations to break the new resolution "just this once." This "just once" idea kills off more good resolutions than any other one cause. The moment you yield "just this once" you introduce the thin edge of the wedge that could, in the end, split your resolution into pieces.

Equally important is the fact that each time you resist temptation, your resolution becomes stronger. Act upon your resolution as early and as often as possible and the stronger it becomes. You are adding to the strength of your original resolution every time you back it up with action.

> *You are adding to the strength of your original resolution every time you back it up with action.*

The mind has been likened to a piece of paper that has been folded. Ever afterwards it tends to fold in the same crease—unless we make a new crease or fold, when it will follow the last lines. The creases are habits—every time we make one it is so much easier for the mind to fold along the same crease afterward. Let us make our mental creases in the right direction.

11

THE PSYCHOLOGY OF EMOTION

||||||||||||||||||||||||||||||||||||||||||||||

We often think the emotions are independent from habit. We easily may think of one acquiring habits of action, and even of thinking, but we usually regard the emotions as something connected with "feeling" and quite divorced from intellectual effort. Yet, notwithstanding the distinction between the two, both are dependent largely upon habit, and one may repress, increase, develop, and change one's emotions, just as one may control habits of action and lines of thought.

It is known in psychology that "emotions deepen by repetition." If a person allows a state of feeling to thoroughly take possession of them, they will find it easier to yield to the same emotion the second time, and so on, until the particular emotion or feeling becomes second nature to them. If an undesirable emotion shows itself inclined to take up a permanent home in your mind, you had better start to work to change it, or at least to master it. And the best time to do this is at the start; for each repetition renders the habit more firmly intrenched, and the task of dislodging it more difficult.

Were you ever jealous? If so, you will remember how insidious was its first approach, how subtly it whispered negative suggestions into your willing ear, and how gradually it followed up such suggestions, until, finally you began to see green. (Jealousy has an effect upon the bile, and causes it to poison the blood. This is why the idea of green is always associated with it.) Then you will remember how the thing seemed to grow, taking possession of you until you scarcely could shake it off. You found it much easier to become jealous the next time. It seemed to bring before you all sorts of objects apparently justifying your suspicions and feeling. Everything began to look green—the green-eyed monster grew.

So it is with every feeling or emotion. If you give way to a fit of rage, you will find it easier to become angry the next time, on less provocation. The habit of feeling and acting "mean" does not take long to firmly settle itself in its new home if encouraged. Worry is a great habit for growing and waxing fat. People start by worrying about big things, and then begin to worry and fret about some smaller thing. And then the merest trifle worries and distresses them. They imagine that all sorts of evil things are about to befall them. If they start on a journey they are certain there is going to be a wreck. If a message comes, it is sure to contain some dreadful tidings. If a child seems a little quiet, the worrying parent is positive it is going to fall ill. If the spouse seems thoughtful, as they resolve some issue in their mind, then the partner is convinced that they are beginning to lose affection. And so it goes—worry, worry, worry—each indulgence making the habit more at home. After a while the continued thought shows itself in action. Not only is the mind poisoned by the destructive thoughts, but we begin to feel the effects of the poison.

The condition of mind known as "fault-finding" is another emotion that grows large with exercise. First, fault is found with this thing, then with that, and finally with everything. The person becomes a chronic "complainer"—a burden to friends and relatives, and someone to be avoided by outsiders. This nagging is all a matter of habit. It grows from small beginnings, and each time it is indulged in it throws out another root, branch, or tendril, and fastens itself closer to the one who has given it soil in which to grow.

Envy, uncharitableness, gossip, scandal-mongering, are all habits of this kind. The seeds are in every human breast, and only need good soil and a little watering to grow stronger.

Each time you give way to one of these negative emotions, the easier you make it for a recurrence of the same thing, or similar ones. Sometimes by encouraging one unworthy emotion, you find that you have given room for the growth of a whole family of these mental weeds.

Now, this is not a good old sermon against the sin of bad thoughts. It is merely a calling of your attention to the law underlying the psychology of emotions. Nothing new about it—old as the hills—so old that many of us have forgotten all about it.

If you wish to manifest these constantly disagreeable and unpleasant traits, and to suffer the unhappiness that comes from them, by all means do so—that is your own business, and your choice. It's none of my business, and I am not preaching at you—it keeps me busy minding my own business and keeping an eye on my own undesirable habits and actions. I am merely telling you how the Law of Attraction works regarding this matter, and you may do the rest.

If you wish to choke out these habits, there are two ways open to you. First, whenever you find yourself indulging in a negative thought or feeling, take ahold of it immediately and say to it firmly, and vigorously, "Get out!" It won't like this at first, and will curve its back and snarl back at you. But never mind—just say "Get out!" to it. The next time it will not be so confident and aggressive—it will have manifested a little of the fear-habit. Each time you repress and choke out a tendency of this kind, the weaker it will become, and the stronger your will becomes.

Professor James says: "Refuse to express a passion, and it dies. Count ten before venting your anger, and its occasion seems ridiculous. Whistling to keep up courage is no mere figure of speech. On the other hand, sit all day in a moping posture, sigh, and reply to everything with a dismal voice, and your melancholy lingers. There is no more valuable precept in moral education than this, as all who have experience know: if we wish to conquer emotional tendencies in ourselves, we must assiduously, and in the first instance, cold-bloodedly, go through the *outward movements* of those contrary dispositions which we prefer to cultivate. Smooth the brow, brighten the eye, contract the dorsal rather than the ventral aspect of the frame, and speak in a major key, pass the genial compliment, and your heart must be frigid indeed if it does not gradually thaw."

12

DEVELOPING NEW BRAIN CELLS

||||||||||||||||||||||||||||||||||||||||||||||||||||||

I have spoken of the plan of getting rid of undesirable states of feeling by driving them out. But a far better way is to cultivate the feeling or emotion directly opposed to the one you wish to eradicate.

We are very apt to regard ourselves as the victims of our emotions and feelings, and to fancy that these feelings and emotions are "who we are." But such is far from being the truth. It is true that the majority of people are at the mercy of their emotions and feelings, and are governed by them to a great degree. They think that feelings are things that rule oneself, and from which one cannot free themself, and so they cease to resist them. They yield to the feeling without question, although they may know that the emotion or mental trait is calculated to injure them, and to bring unhappiness and failure instead of happiness and success. They say "we are made that way," and let it go at that.

The new discoveries in psychology are teaching people better things. It tells them that they are masters of their emotions and feelings instead of being their prisoner. It tells them that brain cells may be developed that will manifest along desirable lines, and that the old brain cells that have been manifesting so unpleasantly may be placed on the retired list and allowed to atrophy from want of use. People may make themselves over and change their entire natures. This is not mere idle theory, but is a working fact which has been demonstrated by countless people, and which is coming more and more before the attention of the public.

No matter what theory of mind we entertain, we must admit that the brain is the organ and instrument of the mind, in our present state of existence, at least, and that the brain must be considered in this matter. The brain is like a wonderful musical instrument, having millions of keys, upon which we may play innumerable combinations of sounds. We come into the world with certain tendencies, temperaments, and predispositions. We may account for these tendencies by heredity, or we may account for them upon theories of pre-existence, but the facts remain the same. Certain keys seem to respond to our touch more easily than others. Certain notes seem to sound forth as the current of circumstances sweeps over the strings. And certain other notes are less easily vibrated. But we find that if we but make an effort of the will to restrain the utterance of some of these easily sounded strings, they will grow more difficult to sound and less liable to be stirred by the passing breeze. And if we will pay attention to some of the other strings that have not been giving forth a clear tone, we will soon get them in good working order; their notes will chime forth clear and vibrant and will drown the less pleasant sounds.

We have millions of unused brain cells awaiting our cultivation. We are using but a few of them, and some of these we are working too much. We are able to give some of these cells a rest by using other cells. The brain may be trained and cultivated in a manner incredible to one who has not looked into the subject. Mental attitudes may be acquired and cultivated, changed and discarded, at will. There is no longer any excuse for people manifesting unnecessary, unpleasant, and harmful mental states. We have the remedy in our own hands.

We acquire habits of thought, feeling, and action, by repeated use.

We acquire habits of thought, feeling, and action, by repeated use. We may be born with a tendency in a certain direction, or we may acquire tendencies by suggestions from others; such as the examples of those around us, suggestions from reading, listening to teachers. We are a bundle of mental habits. Each time we indulge in an undesirable thought or habit, it becomes easier to repeat that thought or action. And the more often we give forth a certain desirable thought, or perform a desirable action, the easier it becomes for us to repeat that thought or action.

Mental scientists are in the habit of speaking of desirable thoughts or mental attitudes as "positive," and of the undesirable ones as "negative." There is a good reason for this. The mind instinctively recognizes certain things as good for the individual to which it belongs, and it clears the path for such thoughts, and interposes the least resistance to them. They have a much greater effect than an undesirable thought possesses, and one positive thought will counteract a number of negative thoughts. The best way to overcome undesirable or negative thoughts and feelings is to cultivate the positive ones. The positive thought is the strongest plant, and will in time starve out the negative one by withdrawing from it the nourishment necessary for its existence.

Of course the negative thought will set up a vigorous resistance at first, for it is a fight for life with it. It sees its finish if the positive thought is allowed to grow and develop; and, consequently, it makes things unpleasant for the individual until that person has started the work of starving it out. Brain cells do not like to be laid on the shelf any more than does any other form of living energy, and they rebel and struggle until they become too weak to do so. The best way is to pay as little attention as possible to these weeds of the mind, but put in as much time as possible watering, caring for, and attending to the new and beautiful plants in the garden of the mind.

For instance, if you are apt to hate people, you can best overcome the negative thought by cultivating Love in its place. Think Love, and act it out, as often as possible. Cultivate thoughts of kindness, and act as kindly as you can to everyone with whom you come in contact. You will have trouble at the start, but gradually Love will master Hate, and the latter will begin to droop and wither. If you have a tendency toward the "blues," cultivate a smile and a more positive view of things. Insist upon your mouth wearing upturned corners, and make an effort of the will to look upon the bright side of things. The "blues" will set up a fight, of course, but pay no attention to them—just go on cultivating optimism and cheerfulness. Let "Bright, Cheerful, and Happy" be your watchword, *and try to live it as fully as you can.*

Thoughts take form in action; and in turn actions influence thought.

These recipes may seem very old and timeworn, but they are psychological truths and may be used by you to advantage. If you once comprehend the nature of the thing, the affirmations and auto-suggestions may be understood and taken advantage of. You may make yourself energetic instead of depleted, active instead of lazy, by this method. It is all a matter of practice and steady work. Positive thinkers often have much to say about "holding the thought"; and, indeed, it is necessary to "hold the thought" in order to accomplish results. But something more is needed. You must "act out" the thought until it becomes a fixed habit with you. Thoughts take form in action; and in turn actions influence thought. So by "acting out" certain lines of thought, the actions react upon the mind, and increase the development of the part of the mind having close relation to the act. Each time the mind entertains a thought, the easier becomes the resulting action—and each time an act is performed, the easier becomes the corresponding thought. So you see the thing works both ways—action and reaction. If you feel cheerful and happy, it is very natural for you to laugh. And if you will laugh a little, you will begin to feel bright and cheerful. Do you see what I am trying to get at? Here it is, in a nutshell: *If you wish to cultivate a certain habit of action, begin by cultivating the mental attitude corresponding to it. And as a means of cultivating that mental attitude, start in to "act-out," or go through, the motions of the act corresponding to the thought.* Now, see if you can apply this rule. Take up something that you really feel should be done, but which you do not *feel* like doing. Cultivate the thought leading up to it—say to yourself: "I like to do so and so," and then go through the motions (cheerfully, remember!) and act out the thought that you like to do the thing. Take an interest in the doing—study out the best way to do it—put brains into it—take a pride in it—and you will find yourself doing the thing with a considerable amount of pleasure and interest—you will have cultivated a new habit.

If you prefer trying it on some mental trait of which you wish to be rid, it will work the same way. Start in to cultivate the opposite trait, and think it out and act it out for all you are worth. Then watch the change that will come over you. Don't be discouraged at the resistance you will encounter at first, but sing gaily: "I Can and I Will," and get to work in earnest. The important thing in this work is to keep cheerful and interested. If you manage to do this, the rest will be easy.

13

THE ATTRACTIVE POWER—DESIRE FORCE

||||||||||||||||||||||||||||||||||||||||||||||||||||

We have discussed the necessity of getting rid of fear, that your desire may have full strength with which to work. Supposing that you have mastered this part of the task, or at least started on the road to mastery, I will now call your attention to another important aspect of the subject. I allude to the subject of mental leaks. No, I don't mean the leakage arising from your failure to keep your own secrets—that is also important, but forms another story. The leakage I am now referring to is that created by the habit of having our attention attracted to, and distracted by, every passing fancy.

In order to attain something it is necessary that the mind should fall in love with it, and be conscious of its existence, almost to the exclusion of everything else. You must get in love with the thing you wish to attain, just as much as you would if you were to meet the person you wished to marry. I do not mean that you should become a monomaniac upon the subject, and should lose all interest in everything else in the world—that won't do, for the mind must have recreation and change. But, I do mean that you must be so "set" upon the desired thing that all else will seem of secondary importance. A person in love may be pleasant to every one else, and may go through the duties and pleasures of life with good spirit, but underneath it all they are humming to themselves about "that certain one," and every one of their actions is bent toward getting that "one," and creating a life together. Do you see what I mean? You must fall in love with the thing you want, and you must get in love with it in earnest—none of this latter-day flirting, "on-today and off-tomorrow" sort of love, but the good old-fashioned kind.

And the person in search of success must make of that desired thing their ruling passion—they must keep their mind on the main chance. Success is jealous—it demands our whole affection. Mental Force operates best when it is concentrated. You must give to the desired thing your best and most earnest thought. Just as the person who is thoroughly in love will think out plans and ways where they may please the one they love, so will the one who is in love with their work or business give it their best thought, and the result will be that a hundred and one plans will come into their field of consciousness, many of which are very important. Remember, the mind works on the subconscious plane, and almost always along the lines of the ruling passion or desire. It will fix up things, and patch together plans and schemes, and when you need them the most it will pop them into your consciousness, and you will feel like shouting "hurrah!", just as if you had received some valuable aid from outside.

However, if you scatter your thought-force, the subconscious mind will not know just how to please you, and the result is that you are apt to be put off from this source of aid and assistance. Beside this, you will miss the powerful result of concentrated thought in the conscious working out of the details of your plans. And then again, the person whose mind is full of a dozen interests fails to exert the attracting power that is manifested by someone who has one ruling passion, and that person also fails to draw to themselves persons, things, and results that will aid in the working out of their plans, and will also fail to place themself in the current of attraction whereby they are brought into contact with those who will be glad to help them because of harmonious interests.

I have noticed, in my own affairs, that when I would allow myself to be side-tracked by anything outside of my regular line of work, it would be only a short time before my receipts dropped off, and my business showed signs of a lack of vitality. Now, many may say that this was because I left undone some things that I would have done if my mind had been centered on the business. This is true; but I have noticed similar results in cases where there was nothing to be *done*—cases in which the seed was sown, and the crop was awaited. And, in just such cases, as soon as I directed my thought to the matter, the seed began to sprout. I do not mean that I had to send out great mental waves with the idea of affecting people—not a bit of it. I simply began to realize what a good thing I had, and how much people wanted it, and how glad they would be to know of it, and all that sort of thing, and lo! my thought seemed to vitalize the work, and the seed began to sprout. This is no mere fancy, for I have experienced it on several occasions; I have spoken to many others on the subject, and I find that our experiences tally perfectly. So don't get into the habit of permitting these mental leaks. Keep your desire fresh and active, and let it get in its work without interference from conflicting desires. Keep in love with the thing you wish to attain—feed your fancy with it—see it as accomplished already, *but don't lose your interest.* Keep your eye on the main chance, and keep your one ruling passion strong and vigorous. Don't be a mental polygamist—one mental love is all that you need—that is, *one at a time.*

> *Keep in love with the thing you wish to attain—feed your fancy with it—see it as accomplished already,* but don't lose your interest. *Keep your eye on the main chance, and keep your one ruling passion strong and vigorous.*

Some scientists have claimed that something that might as well be called "Love" is at the bottom of the whole of life. They claim that the love of the plant for water causes it to send forth its roots until the loved thing is found. They say that the love of the flower for the sun causes it to grow away from the dark places so that it may receive the light. The so-called "chemical affinities" are really a form of love. And desire is a manifestation of this Universal Life Love. So I am not using a mere figure of speech when I tell you that you must love the thing you wish to attain. Nothing but intense love will enable you to surmount the many obstacles placed in your path. Nothing but that love will enable you to bear the burdens of the task. The more desire you have for a thing, the more you Love it;

and the more you Love it, the greater will be the attractive force exerted toward its attainment—both within yourself and outside of you.

So don't divide your energy—love one thing at a time.

14

THE GREAT DYNAMIC FORCES

||||||||||||||||||||||||||||||||||||||||||||||

You have noticed the difference between the successful people in any walk of life, and the less successful people around them. You are conscious of the widely differing characteristics of the two, but somehow find it difficult to express just in what the difference lies. Let us take a look at the matter.

> *Energy and invincible determination—these two things will sweep away mighty barriers, and will surmount the greatest obstacles. And yet they must be used together. Energy without determination will go to waste.*

Energy and invincible determination—these two things will sweep away mighty barriers, and will surmount the greatest obstacles. And yet they must be used together. Energy without determination will go to waste. Lots of people have plenty of energy—they are full to overflowing with it; and yet they lack concentration—they lack the concentrated force that enables them to bring their power to bear upon the right spot. Energy is not nearly so rare a thing as many imagine it to be. I can look around me at any time and pick out a number of people I know who are full of energy—many of them are energy *plus*—and yet, somehow, they do not seem to make any headway. They are wasting their energy all the time. Now they are fooling with this thing—and a day later they are meddling with that. They will take up some thing of no real interest or importance, and waste enough energy and nervous force to carry them through a hard day's work; and yet when they are through, nothing has been accomplished.

Others who have plenty of energy fail to direct it by the power of the Will toward the desired end. "Invincible determination"—those are the words. Do they not thrill you with their power? If you have something to do, get to work and do it. Marshal your energy, and then guide and direct it by your Will—bestow upon it that "invincible determination" and you will do the thing.

Everyone has within them a giant will, but the majority of us are too lazy to use it. We cannot get ourselves nerved up to the point at which we can say, truthfully: *"I Will."* If we can but screw up our courage to that point, and will then pin it in place so that it will not slip back, we will be able to call into play that wonderful power—the Human Will. Humans, as a rule, have but the faintest conception of the power of the Will, but those who have studied along the occult teachings know that the Will is one of the great dynamic forces of the universe, and if harnessed and directed properly it is capable of accomplishing almost miraculous things.

"Energy and Invincible Determination"—aren't they magnificent words? Commit them to memory—press them into your mind, and they will be a constant inspiration to you in hours of need. Say these words over and over again, and see how you are filled with new life—see how your blood will circulate—how your nerves will tingle. Make these words a part of yourself, and then go forth anew to the battle of life, encouraged and strengthened. Put them into practice. "Energy and Invincible Determination"—let that be your motto in your work-a-day life, and you will be one of those rare few who are able to "do things."

Many persons are deterred from doing their best by the fact that they underrate themselves by comparison with the successful ones of life, or rather, overrate the successful ones by comparison with themselves.

One of the curious things noticed by those who are brought in contact with the people who have "arrived" is the fact that these successful people are not extraordinary after all. You meet with some great writer, and you are disappointed to find them very ordinary indeed. They do not converse brilliantly, and, in fact, you know a score of everyday people who seem far more brilliant than this author who dazzles you by their brightness in their books. You meet some great statesman, and they do not seem nearly so wise as a lot of the people in your own village, who waste their wisdom upon the desert air. You meet some great captain of industry, and they do not give you the impression of the shrewdness so marked in some little bargain-driving trader in your own town. How is this, anyway? Are the reputations of these people fictitious, or what is the trouble?

The trouble is this: You have imagined these people to be made of superior metal, and are disappointed to find them made of the same stuff as yourself and those about you. But, you ask, wherein does their greatness of achievement lie? Chiefly in this: Belief in themselves and in their inherent power, in their faculty to concentrate on the work in hand, when they are working, and in their ability to prevent leaks of power when they are not working. *They believe in themselves*, and make every effort count. A wise person in your village spills their wisdom on every corner, and talks to a lot of fools; when if that person was really wise they would save up their wisdom and direct it where it would do some work. The brilliant writer does not waste their wit upon every comer; in fact, they shut the drawer in which they contain their wit, and open it only when they are ready to concentrate and get down to business. The business leader has no desire to impress you with their shrewdness and "smartness." They never did, even when they were young. While their companions were talking instead of doing, this future successful person was doing instead of talking.

The great people of the world—that is, those who have "arrived"—are not very different from you, or me, or the rest of us—all of us are about the same at the base. You have only to meet them to see how very "ordinary" they are, after all. But, don't forget the fact that *they* know how to use the material that is in them; while the rest of the crowd does not, and, in fact, even doubts whether the true stuff is there. The person who "gets there," usually starts out by realizing that they are not so very different, after all, from the successful people that they hear so much about. This gives them confidence, and the result is they find out that they are able to "do things." Then they learn to keep their mouths closed, and to avoid wasting and dissipating their energy. They store up energy, and concentrate it upon the task at hand; while their companions are scattering their energies in every direction, trying to show off and let people know how smart they are. The person who "gets there," prefers to wait for the applause that follows deeds accomplished, and cares very little for the praise that attends promises of what we expect to do "someday," or an exhibition of "smartness" without works.

One of the reasons that people who are thrown in with successful people often manifest success themselves, is that they are able to watch those who are successful and sort of "catch the trick" of their greatness. They see that the successful person is an everyday sort, but that they thoroughly believe in themself, and also that they do not waste energy, but reserves all their force for the actual tasks before them. And, profiting by example, they start to work and put the lesson into practice in their own lives.

Don't undervalue yourself, or overvalue others.

Now what is the moral of this talk? Simply this: Don't undervalue yourself, or overvalue others. Realize that you are made of good stuff, and that locked within your mind are many good things. Then get to work and unfold those good things, and make something out of that good stuff. Do this by attention to the things before you, and by giving to each the best that is in you, knowing that plenty of more good things are in you ready for the fresh tasks that will come. Put the best of yourself into the undertaking on hand, and do not cheat the present task in favor of some future one. Your supply is inexhaustible. And don't waste your good stuff on the crowd of watchers and critics who are standing around watching you work. Save your good stuff for your job or goal, and don't be in too much of a hurry for applause. Avoid the desire to scatter your pearls before—well, before those who only want to be entertained by a "free show."

This teaching may sound like common sense, perhaps, but it is what many of you need very much. Stop fooling, and get down to business. Stop wasting good raw material, and start to work making something worthwhile. This is how you will magnetize yourself in the Law of Attraction.

15

CLAIMING YOUR OWN

IIIIIIIIIIIIIIIIIIIIIIIIIIIIIIIIIIIIIIIIIIIIIIIIIIIII

I n a recent conversation, I was telling a woman to pluck up courage and to reach out for a certain good thing for which she had been longing for many years, and which, at last, appeared to be in sight. I told her that it looked as if her desire was about to be gratified—that the Law of Attraction was bringing it to her. She lacked faith, and kept on repeating, "Oh! It's too good to be true—it's too good for *me!*" She had not emerged from the stage of feeling unworthy, and although she was in sight of the Promised Land she refused to enter it because it "was too *good* for her." I think I succeeded in putting sufficient confidence into her to enable her to claim her own, for the last report I heard of her is that she is accepting her success.

I want to call your attention to the fact that nothing is too good for YOU—no matter how great the thing may be—no matter how undeserving you may mistakenly believe yourself to be. You are entitled to the best there is. So don't be afraid to ask—demand—and take. The good things of the world are not the portion of any favored few. They belong to ALL, but they tend to come only to those who are wise enough to recognize that they deserve the good things, and who are sufficiently courageous to reach out to receive them. Many good things are lost for want of the asking. Many splendid things are lost to you because of your feeling that you are unworthy of them. Many great things are lost to you because you lack the confidence and courage to demand and take possession of them.

"None but the brave deserves the fair," says the old adage, and the rule is true in all lines of human effort. If you keep on repeating that you are unworthy of the good thing—that it is too good for you—the Law of Attraction will be apt to take you at your word and believe what you say. That's a peculiar thing about the Law of Attraction—it believes what you say—it takes you seriously. So beware what you say to it, for it will be apt to give credence. Say to it that you are worthy of the best there is, and that there is nothing too good for you, and you will be likely to have the Law of Attraction take you seriously, and say, "I guess this person is right; I'm going to give them what they want—they know their rights, and what's the use of trying to deny it to him?" But if you say, "Oh, it's too good for *me!*" the Law of Attraction will probably say, "Well, I guess that is so. Surely this person ought to know, and it isn't for me to contradict them." And so it goes.

> *That's a peculiar thing about the Law of Attraction—it believes what you say—it takes you seriously.*

Why should anything be too good for you? Did you ever stop to think just what you are? You are a manifestation of the

Whole Thing, the Absolute, and have a perfect right to all there is. Or, if you prefer it this way, you are a child of the Infinite, and are heir to it all. You are telling the truth in either statement, or both. At any rate, no matter for what you ask, you are merely demanding your own. And the more serious you are about demanding it—the more confident you are of receiving it—the more will you use in reaching out for it—the surer you will be to obtain it.

> *Strong desire—confident expectation—courage in action—these things bring to you your own.*

Strong desire—confident expectation—courage in action— these things bring to you your own. But before you put these forces into effect, you must awaken to a realization that you are merely asking for your own, and not for something to which you have no right or claim. So long as there exists in your mind the last sneaking bit of doubt as to your worthiness for the things you want, you will be setting up a resistance to the operation of the Law of Attraction. You may demand as vigorously as you please, but you will lack the courage to act, if you have a lingering doubt of your right to the thing you want. If you persist in regarding the desired thing as if it belonged to another, instead of to yourself, you will be placing yourself in the position of the covetous or envious person, or even in the position of a tempted thief. In such a case your mind will revolt at proceeding with the work, for it instinctively will recoil from the idea of taking what is not your own—the mind is honest. But when you realize that the best the Universe holds belongs to you as a Divine Heir, and that there is enough for all without your taking something from anyone else, then the friction is removed, and the barrier broken down, and the Law proceeds to do its work.

> *When you realize that the best the Universe holds belongs to you as a Divine Heir, and that there is enough for all without your taking something from anyone else, then the friction is removed, and the barrier broken down, and the Law proceeds to do its work.*

I do not believe in this "humble" business. This meek and lowly attitude does not appeal to me—there is no sense in it, at all. The idea of making a virtue of such things, when each one of us is the heir of the Universe, and is entitled to whatever they need for their growth, happiness, and satisfaction! I do not mean that one should assume a blustering and domineering attitude of mind—that is also absurd, for true strength does not so exhibit itself. The blusterer is a self-confessed weakling—he blusters to disguise his weakness. The truly strong person is calm, self-contained, and carries with them a consciousness of strength which renders unnecessary the bluster and fuss of assumed strength. But get away from this hypnotism of "humility"—this "meek and lowly" attitude of mind. Throw back your head and look the world square in the face. There's nothing to be afraid of—the world is apt to be as much afraid of you, as you are of it, anyway. This applies to your mental attitude, as well as to your outward demeanor. Stop this crawling in your mind. See yourself as standing erect and facing life without fear, and you will gradually grow into your ideal.

There is nothing that is too good for you—not a thing. The

best there is is not beginning to be good enough for you; for there are still better things ahead. The best gift that the world has to offer is a mere bauble compared to the great things in the Cosmos that await you. So don't be afraid to reach out for these playthings of life—these baubles of this plane of consciousness. Reach out for them—grab a whole fistful—play with them until you are tired; that's what they are made for, anyway. They are made for our express use—not to look at, but to be played with, if you desire. Help yourself—there's a whole shopful of these toys awaiting your desire, demand, and taking. Don't be bashful! Don't let me hear any more of this silly talk about things being too good for you. Pshaw! Interestingly, you don't find this trouble with children as a rule. They instinctively recognize that nothing is too good for them. They want all that is in sight to play with, and they seem to feel that the things are theirs by right. And that is the condition of mind that we seekers after the Divine Adventure must cultivate. Unless we become as little children we cannot enter the Kingdom of Heaven.

The things we see around us are the playthings of the Kindergarten of the Infinite, playthings which we use in our game-tasks. Help yourself to them—ask for them without bashfulness—demand as many as you can make use of—they are yours. And if you don't see just what you want, ask for it—there's a big reserve stock on the shelves, enough for everyone. Play, play, play, to your heart's content. Learn to weave mats—to build houses with the blocks—to stitch outlines on the squares—play the game through, and play it well. And demand all the proper materials for the play—don't be bashful—there's enough to go round.

But—remember this! While all this be true, the best things are still only game-things—toys, blocks, mats, cubes, and all

the rest. Useful, most useful for the learning of the lessons—
pleasant, most pleasant with which to play—and desirable,
most desirable, for these purposes. Get all the fun and profit
out of the use of things that is possible. Throw yourself heart-
ily into the game, and play it out—it is Good. But, here's the
thing to remember—never lose sight of the fact that these good
things are but playthings—part of the game—and you must
be perfectly willing to lay them aside when the time comes to
pass into the next class, and not cry and mourn because you
must leave your playthings behind you. Do not allow yourself
to become unduly attached to things—they are for your use
and pleasure, but are not a part of you—not essential to your
happiness in the next stage. Despise them not because of their
lack of Reality—they are great things relatively, and you may as
well have all the fun out of them that you can—don't be a spiritual prude, standing aside and refusing to join in the game. But
do not tie yourself to them—they are good to use and play with,
but not good enough to use *you* and to make *you* a plaything.
Don't let the toys turn the tables on you.

> *Do not allow yourself to become unduly*
> *attached to things—they are for your use*
> *and pleasure, but are not a part of you—not*
> *essential to your happiness in the next stage.*

This is the difference between the Leader of Circumstances
and the Follower of Circumstances. The Follower thinks that
these playthings are real, and that as a follower they are not
good enough to have them. They end up getting only a few toys,
because they are afraid to ask for more, and they miss most
of the fun. And then, considering the toys to be real, and not

realizing that there are plenty more where these came from, they attach themself to the little trinkets that have come their way, and allow themself to be become too attached to them. The follower is afraid that the toys may be taken away from them, and is afraid to toddle across the floor and help themself to the others. The Leader, however, knows that all are theirs for the asking. The Leader demands that which they need from day to day, and does not worry about overloading themself; for they know that there are "lots more," and that they cannot be cheated out of them. They play, and play well, and have a good time in the playing—and learns the Kindergarten lessons in the playing. But they do not become too attached to the toys. They are willing to fling away the worn-out one, and reach out for a new one. And when they are called into the next room for promotion, they drop on the floor the worn-out toys of the day, and with glistening eyes and confident attitude of mind, marches into the next room—into the Great Unknown—with a smile on their face. The Leader is not afraid, for they hear the voice of the Teacher, and knows that the Teacher is there waiting for them—in that Great Next Room.

16

LAW, NOT CHANCE

||||||||||||||||||||||||||||||||||||||||||||||||||||

S ome time ago I was talking to a man about the Attractive
Power of Thought, or the Law of Attraction. He said that
he did not believe that Thought could attract anything to
him, and that it was all a matter of luck. He had found, he said,
that ill luck relentlessly pursued him, and that everything he
touched went wrong. It always had, and always would, and
he had grown to expect it. When he undertook a new thing
he knew beforehand that it would go wrong and that no good
would come of it. Oh, no! There wasn't anything in the theory
of Attractive Thought, so far as he could see; it was all a matter
of luck!

This man failed to see that by his own confession he was
giving a most convincing argument in favor of the Law of Attraction. He was testifying that he was always expecting things
to go wrong, and that they always came about as he expected.
He was a magnificent illustration of the Law of Attraction—
but he didn't know it, and no argument seemed to make the

matter clear to him. He was "up against it," and there was no way out of it—he always expected the bad luck, and every occurrence proved that he was right, and that the Mental Science position was all nonsense.

There are many people who seem to think that the only way in which the Law of Attraction operates is when one *wishes* hard, strong, and steady. They do not seem to realize that a strong *belief* is as effective as a strong wish. The successful person believes in themselves and is confident in their ultimate success. They pay no attention to little setbacks, stumbles, tumbles, and slips. They press on eagerly to the goal, believing all the time that they will get there. Their views and aims may alter as they go along, and they might change their plans or have them changed for them, but all the time they know in their heart that they will eventually "get there." They are not steadily *wishing* they may get there—they simply *feel* it and *believe* it, and thereby set into operation the strongest forces known in the world of thought.

The person who just as steadily believes they are going to fail will invariably fail. How could they help it? There is no special miracle about it. Everything they do, think, and say is infused with the thought of failure. Other people catch this negative spirit, and fail to trust this person or their ability, which this person then chooses to believe is just more of their bad luck instead of crediting these results to their own belief and expectation of failure. This person is suggesting failure to themselves all the time, and will invariably take on the effect of this powerful autosuggestion. This person by their own negative thoughts shuts up that portion of their mind from which should come the ideas and plans conducive to success, that same part of the mind which sends ideas and plans to the one who does expect success because they believe in it. A state of discouragement is not the ideal state of mind in which bright ideas may come to us. It is when we are enthused and hopeful that our mind will work out the very ideas which we may turn to success.

Clear up your Mental Atmosphere!

There is no such thing as chance. The Law of Attraction maintains everything and is everywhere. All that happens happens because of the operation of Law of Attraction. You cannot name the simplest thing that ever occurred by chance—try it, and then trace the thing down to a final analysis, and you will see it as the result of Law of Attraction. It is as plain as mathematics. Plan and purpose; cause and effect. From the movements of worlds to the growth of the grain of mustard seed—all the result of natural laws. The fall of the stone down the mountain-side is not chance—natural laws and forces which had been in operation for centuries caused it. And back of that cause were other causes, and so on until the Causeless Cause is reached.

Life is not the result of chance—the Law is here, too. The Law is in full operation whether you know it or not—whether you believe in it or not. You may be the ignorant object upon which the Law of Attraction operates, and bring yourself all sorts of trouble because of your ignorance of or opposition to the Law. Or you may fall in alignment with the operations of the Law—get into its current, as it were—and Life will seem a far different thing to you. You cannot get outside of the Law by refusing to have anything to do with it. You are at liberty to oppose it and produce all the friction you wish to—it doesn't hurt the Law, and you may keep it up until you learn your lesson.

The Law of Thought Attraction is one name for the Law, or rather for one manifestation of it. Again I say, your thoughts are real things. They go forth from you in all directions, combining with thoughts of like kind—opposing thoughts of a different character—forming combinations—going where they are attracted—flying away from thought centers opposing them. And your mind attracts the thoughts of others, which have been sent out by them consciously or unconsciously. But it attracts only those thoughts which are in harmony with its own. Like attracts like, and opposites repel opposites, in the world of thought.

> *You are today setting into motion thought currents which will in time attract toward you thoughts, people, and conditions in harmony with the predominant note of your thought.*

If you set your mind to the vibration of courage, confidence, strength, and success, you attract to yourself thoughts of like nature; people of like nature; things that fit in the mental tune. Your prevailing thought or mood determines that which is to be drawn toward you—picks out your mental bedfellow. You are today setting into motion thought currents which will in time attract toward you thoughts, people, and conditions in harmony with the predominant note of your thought. Your thought will mingle with that of others of like nature and mind, and you will be attracted toward each other, and will surely come together with a common purpose sooner or later, unless one or the other of you should change the current of their thoughts.

Set your mind to the vibration of courage, confidence, and success.

Fall in alignment with the operations of the Law. Make it a part of yourself. Get into its currents. Maintain your self-control. Set your mind to the vibration of courage, confidence, and success. Get in touch with all the thoughts of that kind that are emanating every hour from countless other minds. Get the best that is to be had in the thought world. The best is there, so be satisfied with nothing less. Get into partnership with good minds. Get into the right vibrations. Are you tired of being tossed about by using the operations of the Law of Attraction negatively? If so, then instead get into harmony with it and see positive results. Become the Law of Attraction in action!

ABOUT THE AUTHOR

||||||||||||||||||||||||||||||||||||||||||||||||

WILLIAM WALKER ATKINSON (1862–1932) was a noted occultist and pioneer of the New Thought Movement. He wrote extensively throughout his lifetime, often using various pseudonyms. He is widely credited with writing *The Kybalion* and was the founder of the Yogi Publication Society.